Going Home

Good Hunting

Robert Hite Neill

Going Home

by ROBERT HITT NEILL

with artwork by
BOB TOMPKINS

MISSISSIPPI RIVER PUBLISHING CO.   Leland, Mississippi

Printed in Japan
Designed and produced by JoAnne Prichard

Library of Congress Cataloging-in-Publication Data

Neill, Robert Hitt.
   Going home.

   1. Hunting—Mississippi.   2. Outdoor life—
Mississippi.   I. Title.
SK95.N45 1987   799.29762'4   87-20225
ISBN 0–9617591–2–7

MISSISSIPPI RIVER PUBLISHING CO.
P.O. Box 896
Leland, MS 38756

Also available from Mississippi River Pub.:
The Flaming Turkey, ISBN 0-9617591-0-0,
   cloth, $17.95
How to Lose Your Farm in Ten Easy Lessons and
   Cope with It, ISBN 0-9617591-1-9, $6.95

This book is dedicated to
BETSY
Because I love her
For better, for worse
For richer, for poorer
In sickness and in health
Till death do us part.

And besides that, she lets me go hunting pretty much
when I want to and doesn't hassle me about it.

Contents

Color plates follow pages 34 and 118.

Acknowledgments

As Bob Tompkins, after reading this manuscript, so wisely said (and I hope you can appreciate this; wise artists are hard to come by, and this one ain't wise all the time.): "This ain't a huntin' book; it's another book about friendship!"

So I acknowledge with thankfulness the friends who have enriched my life with their presence over the years. I will not enumerate them here; that would be just a dry recitation of names. My hope is that you will emerge from the other side of this book feeling that you have met these men; that they have brought pleasure, laughter, and tears to your life; and that you, too, know them well.

A man named Tommy Redus, whom I have never met (and who did not owe me money), called me long distance after finishing *The Flaming Turkey* and said, "I wish I could have shaken Big Robert's hand, because I feel like I know him now." Bless his little heart, I hope Tommy limits out on turkeys for the next ten years.

Now hold still; here come some good friends I want you to get to know. . . .

Forewarning: /$$&*/!!!

When *The Flaming Turkey* was written and published, I had assumed that it would appeal mostly to adult male hunters. I was pleasantly surprised with the success of the book and the fact that it was enjoyed by all kinds of people, from eighty-year-old saintly great-grandmothers to non-hunting preachers, house-wives, and grammar school children.

I was a little perturbed, however, when a youngster told me, "I read some of your chapters to my fourth grade class and they really liked them, especially the one about the Tom and the Buck. But I had to leave out a couple of the words," he added as an afterthought.

"Lordamercy!" I thought. "Am I contributing to the delinquency of minors here? Have I embarassed my saintly aunt or my preacher?" I rushed to a copy of the immoral volume and began to flip through the pages.

Well, I finally decided that it wasn't as bad as all that. Admittedly, there were a few "hells" and "damns" scattered about; several epithets that would more accurately describe male puppies; and one or two other nouns I might have found a substitute for, had I anticipated the extent of my audience.

Let me pause here to speak to the non-hunting world. Let's get it out in the open: hunters on hunting camp sometimes say bad words. Not necessarily in every breath, mind you, and not necessarily every hunter. But some do let their hair down a little, so to speak. Some tell dirty jokes. Some even drink alcoholic beverages, mostly in the evening. I am aware that by revealing these sins, I may be ostracized by hunting groups everywhere. So be it, then. I'll take up preaching.

Knowing all these things, I had sat down with my six-year-old son before he joined me for his first deer camp and had a man-to-man talk with him.

"Son," I said, "you are going to camp with a bunch of men. You may hear words that you are not old enough either to understand or repeat. You will not *be* old enough to repeat these words until you are big enough to whip me. Until that time, if I ever hear you say any cusswords, I will take a belt to you and blister your bottom. I want you to have a good time, but you must understand this part of it. Do you?"

"Yes, Sir," he nodded, big-eyed. And he did. His bottom had been blistered prior to that time, and has been since, but not for cussing. I don't mean to brag, but in the twelve years since that initial speech (it's been given several times a year) I have only heard the boy cuss twice.

Once it was just barely audible, and the occasion was certainly suitable. A big copperhead had just struck me at the top of my boot and my own vocal cords seemed to be paralyzed. I actually appreciated the kid trying to help me express a little of what I undoubtedly would have said had not my mouth been struck totally devoid of moisture.

The second time was a few years later when I was accompanying him on his Sunday morning country paper route. It was a bad foggy morning and I was busy folding papers when I heard an unaccustomed expletive from the young driver. I looked up to see a "T" intersection appear with a light pole and a soybean field on the other side. There was no doubt we couldn't make the turn and that the youngster had done an inadequate job of describing the situation. I proceeded to do so after we had come to a stop several rows over, thankfully with no damage to us or the car.

At any rate, having examined the profanity in *The Flaming Turkey,* I immediately plunged into the research necessary to determine whether to recall the book. I watched a couple of weeks of prime time television; I checked out several popular movies; I went to the library and read articles in leading magazines and newspapers; while there, I leafed through the top ten best-selling books; I scanned my children's assigned book reading lists for school; I listened to and watched popular singers.

Parents, I have come to the conclusion that *The Flaming Turkey* does not even come close to undermining the morals of the youth of America.

Now, as to *Going Home,* let me warn you of what to expect as compared to my aforementioned research.

During this research, I came across vocal, visual, and printed descriptions of sexual activity that left me pop-eyed, short of breath, and sweaty. Though there was some mention of sex in *The Flaming Turkey,* we will steer clear of it in *Going Home.* I am not against sex in its proper place and partner, you will understand, nor am I totally ignorant and unappreciative of it. I just don't write about it very much.

All of us have heard the expression "cussing like a sailor," but I spent two years in the Navy, and I found words in some of these research materials that I completely missed in my tour of duty. Perhaps they have been invented since then. These words will not be found printed in this book.

There are words that describe certain parts of the body, and the functions of these members. We will not use those words in this book. If it becomes necessary to discuss this type thing, we will attempt to do it scientifically and tastefully.

There are terms that refer to the rearward anatomies of livestock that you probably hear daily on the streets, especially when applied to politicians. Some of you may be applying one of these terms to this chapter. Though I may heartily agree with the first application and heartily disagree with the second, you will not find those words in this book.

Some of you may find it hard to believe, but there were pictures, both moving and still, in some of these research materials that portrayed art forms that the average run-of-the-mill citizen would not want his minister to catch him looking at. I diligently examined some of these forms very closely, attempting to find some redeeming literary value. Finding none, we decided not to put any pictures like that in this book.

Now, you may find a few "hells" and "damns" in these pages. I believe that hell is a very real place and many people will go there. If you also believe this, use the occasion afforded by that word in this book to think on that subject and insure that you have made other arrangements for your post-mortem travel. If you don't believe in hell, then it ain't a cussword to you and you ought not to object to its presence in this book. However, I will encourage you to become better informed lest you end up an authority on the place.

"Damn" is a rather mild expletive, in my opinion, and will occasionally be used. If your sensitivities necessitate it, I herewith and in advance apologize to you. My grandmother forbade my grandfather to cuss but Doctor became so expert and emphatic with "Dadblame it!" that everybody knew he was cussing anyway. And I dimly remember a television commercial in my youth when the guy swore "Brasterfrateraster!" and there was no doubt he was cussing.

In direct quotes there may be an instance of a rather descriptive term for male pups. But only if I feel that the deletion of the phrase prevents the reader from getting the full intent of the anger and disgust of the speaker.

You *will* find in this book a continuation of a story that is, unashamedly, a love story. I had not realized that I was putting that emotion on paper in *The Flaming Turkey* until I was introduced at a speaking program by Frank Powers. In the interest of modesty, I will just quote him, to the best of my memory: "You have heard this book advertised as a hunting book. But I want to tell you I have read the book, and what comes across to me is the love and comraderie shared by a group of men who hunt together."

Thanks, Frank.

At any rate, now you know right up front whether to continue reading, or whether to let your grandmother or your child peruse this volume. If you've raised them right, it will not have any detrimental effects.

For instance, my son and I were headed for deer camp one November afternoon when he was about fourteen. "Son," I began, "you are going to camp . . ."

"I know, Daddy," he interrupted. "with a bunch of men. I am going to hear words that I am not old enough. . . ."

"Hell, never mind!" I interrupted in turn, slowing the truck. "You want to drive the rest of the way?"

The Road Back

The Trail Watcher smiled grimly, careful not to bare his teeth. Major Linn had been right: you could smell the round-eyes before you could see them. He nestled deeper into his hole and caressed the switch. "Look for the antenna," he thought. "Major Linn said the officer is always close to the radio."

Mack inhaled deeply, silently, through his nostrils. Gunny Grimes had been right: you could smell the dinks before you saw them. "Durn his time," he cursed under his breath. The reason Mack walked point so much at night was that the old gunnery sergeant had bragged on the Alabaman's nose. "Best smeller in the whole battalion!" he had boasted to Captain Smiley and Lieutenant Turnbull. And now Turnbull, nicknamed "Lt. Turrible" by Mack and the other southerner in the platoon, Mississippi Micky, picked Mack for the point on nearly every night patrol.

"Aw, Lt. Turrible," he had moaned tonight, "there ain't nuthin' I hate wuss'n a night patrol 'cept walkin' point on a night patrol. And the only thing I hate wuss'n that is walkin' point on a trail on a night patrol!"

"Well, we're taking the trail," the officer said firmly. "It's only a klick and a quarter and I want to get there quick and set up before Charlie does. If it'll help your pucker factor any, I'll walk your slack."

"Druther have The Mick, if I had my druthers," Mack had muttered under his breath. Still, Lt. Turrible was about as good as the Mississippi Marine.

He turned to the Lieutenant now and breathed into his ear, "I smell dinks. I b'lieve they're set up for us."

3

"Hold up," Turnbull whispered, "Lemme get The Mick up with the starlight scope."

He passed the word back to Appleton, the radioman, who relayed it to Smitty. Micky was next in the file.

"Starlight up!" Smitty spoke in his ear. "Mack smells Charlie."

Micky eased quietly by the three marines. Lt. Turrible was silently draping his poncho over his and Appleton's heads to muffle his call to the patrol's artillery support with their present coordinates. Appleton slipped the whip antenna loop out of his belt.

The silence was shattered by a tremendous explosion.

A hot blast of wind lifted Micky off his feet and a fiery shock gripped his midsection. His right arm went numb and seemed to fling itself over his head of its own volition. Smitty's boot slammed into his temple, still laced tightly to the lower half of the man's leg. He was catapulted head over heels into a clump of brush. The blackness was slashed by red tracers and hundreds of tiny white winks. "Kinda pretty, like lightnin' bugs back home," he thought. Then he realized it was rifle fire and he couldn't hear it.

A face appeared in front of him, dimly illuminated by tracer fire. Mack. The big guy had made it. He saw the Alabaman's mouth working. "I can't hear you," he said, and couldn't hear himself. "I can't hear!" he screamed.

A big right hand clamped over his mouth, and Mack dragged him out of the bush into a shallow depression. "Help me!" the Alabama boy mouthed and pointed at the stump of his left arm, blood coming in spurts from it.

Together, with Mack's right hand and Micky's left, they managed to get a tourniquet tight and staunch the blood flow. The Mississippian's right arm was still numb, but not bleeding too much from the wound just below his shoulder. He pulled up his fatigue shirt and directed Mack's attention to the jagged wound below the breastbone, seeping dark blood. Mack drew his lips back in

4

an exaggerated grimace and awkwardly extracted a battle dressing and pressed it to the wound. He shrugged at Mick. They both knew it was bad.

The fight was drawing closer to them. "Gimme your grenades," Mack started to say, then realized Micky couldn't hear him. He gently extracted the grenades from his buddy's belt, careful of the stomach wound. "You can't throw them left-handed!" he pantomimed. Micky held up one finger. Mack nodded grimly; he hadn't thought about not being able to pull the pins without his own left hand. He slipped the ring over the outstretched finger, and Mickey curled it and jerked the pin out.

"Yeee-Haaa!" Mack screamed, and heaved the grenade at the closest white firefly.

He was still holding the last grenade at daylight, when Delta's other two platoons arrived to rescue their mates. Doc Ludlow sadly shook his head at the sight of the Alabaman's chalk-white face. "Why didn't you get a couple more with that last one?" he asked as he set up some plasma.

Mack opened one eye. "That 'un's mine and Micky's," he explained tiredly.

Captain Smiley turned to his radioman. "Get that medevac chopper in here ASAP. Tell 'em we got two goin' straight to Danang. We'll tote the rest in," he added grimly; "they're in no hurry."

Doc Ludlow gently uncurled The Mick's finger from the pin of the last grenade and lifted it out of Mack's right hand. The two boys, one eighteen and one nineteen, finally succumbed to unconsciousness as they were lifted into the chopper.

The corpsman boosted himself into the medevac between the wounded marines. "Lemme go in with 'em, Cap'n," he called, "I need to get some plasma into Mack bad."

Captain Smiley waved his assent and ducked away from the rotor wash. The wind from the rising helicopter parted the foliage in front of him, revealing a

5

jungle boot with half a leg still in it. He picked it up and tossed it toward the nearest soldier with a body bag.

"Dammit to hell, anyway!" Captain Smiley growled, and brushed away the tears.

Dove Season 1970

"One of the nicer things about being deaf is that you don't have to answer telephones," thought Micky, as Lisa hurried past his chair toward the phone on the kitchen wall. Thirty seconds later a spoon whizzed over his left shoulder and splatted in the middle of his paper. He turned his attention to his wife.

"Micky, it's Bob," she half-yelled, enunciating each word carefully, "He wants to know if we're coming up for Opening Weekend?"

"Tell him 'no thanks,' " he matched her tone; "ain't no way I can shoot like this."

Lisa relayed that message, listened a minute, and leaned back into the den. "He says you never could shoot anyway, so you'll save lots of money on shells," she laughed. "He says come to see everybody again and for the party."

"Tell him 'no thanks,' " Micky repeated, and turned back to his paper. How the hell could he handle a shotgun again when he could hardly manage to unfold newspaper pages with his right hand?

"Wait a minute," Lisa spoke into the receiver and laid it down. She stepped into the den and knelt by Micky's chair and addressed him pleadingly.

"Mick, I'd really like to go again, and I know you'd enjoy seeing everybody. Come on, Bob's your friend."

"Then tell him 'no thanks, friend'!" he said levelly, and turned off his hearing aid.

She sighed, shrugged, and walked back to the phone. "Bob, he says thanks a lot, but we can't make it this year. But next year we'll be there for sure!" She

6

listened a minute. "Okay, I'll tell him. You be sure and let us know how everything goes and who was there. Tell them 'hi' for us. And Bob," she paused, "Thanks. Thanks a lot. He needs to come."

Dove Season, 1971

Lisa had started her campaign two months before and had gone from enthusiastic encouragement through pleading, cajoling, and bribery, finally to the nagging stage—but she had won!

"All right, dammit!" he had roared. "We'll go. But I ain't takin' no gun. There's no sense in being humiliated. I'll sit in a corner and read while you have your fun."

"Yeah," she teased, "I'll tell all the old crowd I ran you off and got a new guy. Most of them won't know you anyway with your beard and with most of your hair fallen out."

"I'm goin' off the air," he retorted. "I don't have to take this," and he turned his hearing aid off.

She bent and kissed his ear and spoke in it. "Okay, but thanks. I'm glad we're goin' back."

Dove Season was opening on Labor Day weekend, so we were looking forward to having a house full of company from Friday night until Monday afternoon. Betsy had been cooking and freezing for three weeks, about the same length of time I had been working on the dove field. No matter how many doves I had, it always seemed like the first cold front would move through a couple of days before the season and the homegrown doves would migrate out. But Friday was hot and dry, with the same forecast for the weekend.

Thursday night I had started two venison hindquarters over a sassafras fire, added more coals at midnight, and more again at daylight. By the time the first early arrivals came in Friday night, we were ready for Opening Day.

Dove Season in the South is not so much a hunting occasion as it is a social occasion. We usually field about seventy-five to a hundred guns during the afternoon, and have a hundred and fifty folks for the party that Saturday night. Of course, a lot are local friends, but there is a core group of about twenty-five couples from out of town—several a five or six hour drive—that are the best of friends and have hunted together for years.

Sure, I see each one of them at least a couple of times a year, and several of them see several of the others during the rest of the year, but there is only one time a year when we are all together for a weekend, and that is Opening Day at the Plantation. Nine or ten couples usually stay at the family houses here on the Place on a "first call, first come" basis, and the rest resolve to call earlier next year and go to motels in town. There's not a lot of sleeping done anyway. Everybody arrives with food and drink here at the house and it's one long social gathering from Friday night until late Monday.

I guess this is when we celebrate New Year's. The year doesn't change maybe, but dove season signals the start of the hunting seasons that will then be open for some variety of game until the first of May, except for a couple or three weeks in early March between quail and turkey seasons. Opening Weekend is the time when Gary gets a deer hunt arranged with me; when Beau wrangles a duck hunting invitation out of Teddy; when Dude sets up a redfish expedition with Gene; when Gary talks to Russ and Charlie about getting together to shoot ducks or catch bass on Toledo Bend; when Billy and Semmes speculate on a bow hunt for deer; when Mountain Willy tells us all again that his cabin is almost finished. While the hunting arrangements for the next year are made, everybody sits around the house, or the dove field, or the Swimming Hole, or the general store on the Place to share experiences, tell lies, relive old (and getting better!) stories, and just shoot the bull. The wives are

8

just as much a part of this as the husbands. I think what we're actually celebrating is being good friends and caring for each other.

At any rate, this was the kind of atmosphere that Micky and Lisa had missed for a few years. They arrived late Saturday morning, and true to his word, Micky found a corner while Lisa joined the fun.

That afternoon during the hunt, my routine as host was to take people to the field, come back to the house for late arrivals, take them to the field, return to the house for shells for the overconfident ones who had only taken one box, take them to the field, bring out a couple of hot guns who had gotten early limits or maybe heat stroke, load up an ice chest of drinks—in other words, I was back and forth all afternoon. French Gun was in the truck, but I knew I wouldn't have time to use it.

On one of these trips back to the field, I talked The Mick into joining me. As we made the circuit of hunters, offering cold drinks and water, he was effusively greeted by lots of old friends, and seemed to loosen up. By the time we got to the old right-of-way through the woods, he was looking forward to whomever was next, and, when he saw Mr. Hurry, he bailed out of the truck on his own so the older man wouldn't have to walk to us.

This was too good an opportunity to miss. Semmes was getting some water, so I pulled out French Gun and a box of shells. "Here. Keep these for Micky. I'm gonna go off and leave him for a while."

Semmes looked at me dubiously. "He still got the mullygrubbs?"

"I b'lieve he's comin' out a little," I replied, and drove off.

An hour later, Dude, Semmes, and Mr. Hurry were all sitting together when I drove up. Micky was seventy-five yards away but started toward the truck when I stopped to talk to the three hunters.

"You sho' did that boy bad!" fussed Dude.

"How's that?" I asked.

9

"You left the full choke barrel on French Gun," Dude said, and Semmes chimed in. "Yeah, he's so frustrated by now he couldn't hit a bull in the butt with a bass fiddle!"

"Some friend! You know what you did to me?" bellowed the bearded one as he approached.

"Hell, the way you used to shoot, it wouldn't have made any difference if I'da had all three barrels on at the same time!" I retorted.

"I saw he had left the full choke on, but I thought being a Marine, you wanted that so you could shoot your doves in the head!" Semmes spoke as mildly as possible when yelling at someone who can't hear.

"Myself, I didn't figure a Marine could even shoot a gun that wasn't full automatic!" Dude had been a Sneaky Pete and never missed a chance to gig Micky or Gary.

"You guys shoulda seen him the first time he shot. He'd forgot to cut his hearing aid off!" Mr. Hurry laughed. All of this conversation was carried on at a level that included the whole twenty-five acres. There's no sense in agitating somebody unless he's hearing you.

"Sho' nuff, Mick," I apologized, "I'm real sorry. I shoulda looked 'fore I put it in the truck."

"I did get one, though, and I ain't even shot alla that box!" Micky pulled the dove out and held it up proudly.

"Aw Riiiight!" Semmes and I cheered.

"You gonna have it mounted?" Dude yelled innocently, then took off around the truck as the big Marine mock-charged him.

"Here, here, you guys. Peace!" Mr. Hurry hollered. He reached into his own ice chest and pulled out a double handful of little brown bottles. "Let's have a toast to the best job of shooting in the field today!"

"Y'all finish those and come on in," I instructed. "Hunt's over, and the girls

10

say we got to shower before we can party."

There are no corners in the house at the Opening Day Party. After you've checked out all the pretty girls in one room, you circulate to another, always passing by the dining room to refill your plate or the kitchen to replenish your glass. I even found three ladies in conversation in the bathroom that night, one perched on the side of the bathtub, one on the counter, one on the dressing stool, all with plates on their laps.

I am partially deaf myself, so I know how hard it is to hear when there is a lot of background noise. At intervals during the evening, whole rooms of conversation would be halted by a raucous, booming voice. "You talkin' to me?"

By midnight, the crowd was down to about twenty of us in the den laughing at Lisa's rendition of the Cajun saga of Little Rabbit Foo-Foo. Micky was not among us. He had sought out a bed, gone "off the air" and flaked out. There are some times when deafness can be used to your advantage.

What I really want to tell you about happened on the second day hunt, which wasn't even on my place. Mr. David had a grove of medium-sized pecan trees between which he had planted browntop millet. He had cut the millet and baled it for hay, and the bare ground was covered with millet seed—and doves.

We scared the doves up when we arrived and spread out, but not for long. They came back in droves, and it was tough shooting. The trees were just high enough and the doves flying just low enough that you only got snap shots at the grey darters. The best method of locating targets was to listen to your neighbor shoot and to get ready in case he missed. And of course, we all yelled warnings to each other.

Dude had a hot fence corner and was hot himself. He limited out quickly, but was obviously holding his spot. He leaned his breeched sixteen gauge against a fencepost, draped his shell vest from the barbed wire, and left his stool when he walked back toward the truck. I was beginning to move toward his corner when he reappeared lugging a big red cooler, Micky on its other handle.

Dude directed the placement of the cooler in the shade a few steps behind his stool, extracted a small brown bottle from it, grabbed Micky's shoulder, and propelled him toward the fence corner. Then he ceremoniously presented the ex-Marine with his sixteen gauge and shell vest, perched him on the stool, situated himself behind Mick, took a swig from the brown bottle, and announced, "It's already trained. All you got to do is point and pull the trigger!"

Micky was about to protest when Russ called from the trees to their left, "Watch, Dude!"

Dude punched Micky's left shoulder and pointed. A pair of doves zipped across the clearing and Micky instinctively swung and shot. The doves continued their journey. "Don't teach my gun no bad habits!" Dude yelled, and slapped Micky on the head with his cap.

Mick was turning to reply when Gary shot twice out front to the right. Dude punched the brawny right shoulder in front of him and pointed. Another miss. "You can shoot more than once!" Dude said in an aggrieved tone.

"You talkin' to me?" Mick turned his head and bellowed.

Dude leaned down into his face and held up three fingers in front of the beard. "Read my lips," he enunciated, "it's-got-three-shells-in-it!"

Russ shot from the left and yelled right behind the report, "Dude!"

Another punch and point. Three doves jinked through the clearing. The third shot extracted two tail feathers from the trailing bird. "You're gettin' closer," encouraged the pointer, "you want me to pick 'em up?"

The deaf one grunted and cast a baleful eye over his shoulder as he reloaded. Gene's big double barrel boomed from out front at two high doves, and one

12

jerked and set his wings in a long death glide. "Dude! Mark my bird!" Gene yelled.

Dude punched and pointed. The second dove, as they will often do, had followed its wounded companion almost to earth, then flared up. It seemed to hang over the fence corner like a sofa pillow. The sixteen barked and the dove crumpled in a cloud of feathers. "Fetch!" the bearded hunter ordered his retriever, who had already set his brown bottle on the ice box and was climbing through the fence. Seldom have I observed so enthusiastic a retrieve.

Gene appeared at the other end of the clearing and waved at Micky. The hearing aid was turned up and we all heard the familiar refrain, "You talkin' to me?"

Gene bellowed, "Good shot! How bout gettin' your ugly dog to fetch mine, too!"

"Sure!" was the reply. He winked at Dude as his dove was handed over the fence. "Now, fetch!" he ordered, and gave Dude a line. The obedient retriever, tongue lolling, galloped out to the other dove, picked it up, and brought it straight back to the fence corner. His bearded master patted him on the head and handed him the beaded brown bottle.

"Hey! That's my dove!" protested Gene.

"Gitchew a dawg!" was the laughing reply.

Gene shook his fist at the fence corner comedy team and retreated into the trees. Dude resumed his post behind Micky, who turned his hearing aid back down. The punch and point routine began again.

Gene reappeared shortly, having powdered a double for his limit. He ambled up to the red cooler, shucked his vest, laid the broken double barrel on it, and extracted two dripping brown bottles from the box. Handing one to Dude, he took a swig from his and stepped up behind Mick. Dude collapsed into the

13

shade by the ice box. As far as I could tell, not a word was passed between them. Gene's first punch and point produced a kill. "Hey, all you've needed was a good coach!" he yelled to Micky. They both cheered Dude's retrieve.

A shout from Gary provided direction, but the two shots only produced a handful of feathers. "You've forgotten everything I ever taught you," Gene protested.

Fifteen minutes of coaching by Gene had produced a couple more doves when Micky ran his hand into the vest and withdrew the last five shells. "Hey," he hollered at Dude in belligerent astonishment, "There's no more shells in this vest!"

"Yeah, the damn thing leaks," Dude observed loudly, "I've had it do that with me." He hauled himself to his feet and started toward the truck. The sixteen spoke twice.

"Better hurry," called Gene.

Dude returned with shells just as Gary was climbing back through the fence with his limit. "Let's stop summa this dadblame noise over here!" he demanded at the top of his voice. "Feller can't hear himself think!" He spied the red cooler. "Here, what's in that there ice box?" was delivered in the same loud Arkansas twang.

"Keep outta that cooler!" instructed Mick. "That's for my coach and retriever."

"Listen," Gary declared, "us jungle bunnies gotta stick together. Set them two Sneaky Petes down." He pulled a bottle from the chest and stepped behind the hunter as Dude and Gene retreated into the shade.

For the next half box of shells those of us within earshot (the surrounding twenty acres!) were treated to a number of colorful comparisons of the Marine Corps and the Green Berets. All arguments were finally settled by a spectacular double. Gary took credit for coaching, Micky for shooting, Dude for the gun,

14

and Gene for the retrieve. About then Russ walked up and opened the cooler.

"Git outta there!" Gary shoved the top down on his hand. "you know the rules: no beer until you're through huntin'!"

"I'm through! I'm through!" Russ squeezed a bottle out.

"You can't kid us," Dude snorted. "We been watchin' you shoot!"

"Yeah," agreed Gene, "you ain't got as many as Micky."

"Musta been huntin' next to Beau and pickin' up his cripples and floaters," Gary nudged Micky.

"Hey, I don't need this! There's lots of trees in this pasture." Russ made as if to pick up his breeched Remington.

"Nah, stay here and we'll try to get The Mick to give you some tips," Dude promised loudly.

"Would you, oh Great White Hunter?" Russ begged, looking suitably humble.

Micky grinned and nodded, and Russ stepped up behind him, punched and pointed at a right-to-lefter.

As other hunters made their way back to the trucks with limits, they settled on shaded tailgates with cool beverages and kept score by the alternating cheers and jeers from the Peanut Gallery at the fence corner. Beau was coaching when the twelfth dove went down and a roar went up from the trucks as I made the retrieve. The ground was covered with purple hulls.

"Now can I have a beer?" the triumphant hunter asked plaintively.

"There ain't no more!" kidded Gary, and we all laughed at Mick's expression.

Russ dug a little brown bottle from the ice. "If you'll carry this, the rest of us will see if we can get all your game back to the trucks."

The bearded, sunburned hunter led his noisy bearers to the congratulatory crowd at the vehicles.

Supper that night was a seated dinner at the big dining room table. Micky and Lisa had brought rock lobster tails, Gene and Maggie brought boiled shrimp, Billy and Pat a ham, and Betsy and I had charcoaled a platter of big bass. Dude and Gin and Gary and Ann chipped in with vegetables and desserts. Russ had provided most of the little brown bottles during the afternoon, but saved a couple of jugs of wine for the evening.

Micky was seated in the middle on the right, and could not have missed a scrap of conversation. Even if Gene was speaking to Betsy next to him at the end of the table, the neighbors a quarter mile away could have repeated their conversation. It was not a planned thing, and I would not attempt to explain it. But the deaf Marine was an integral part of the group and by the time coffee and brandy were served there was not a happier nor hoarser group to be found anywhere.

Our guests departed the next afternoon, amid hugging and kissing and promises to get back together soon. Betsy and I cleaned up in our usual after-the-Opening-Weekend state of euphoria.

Three months later, Lisa penned on the bottom of their Christmas card: "Micky's finally on the road back. He started Dove Season!"

Advice to a
Hunter's Wife

Just like any young couple who had dated for a few years, then had a fairly long engagement period, we received lots of good advice before we got married. All of it was free, and some was proverbially worth what it cost, but several axioms were excellent, and we have used them for twenty years.

Big Dave's favorite was "the way to handle a woman is to keep her pregnant and barefoot," which didn't work out at all. But his mother-in-law, Miss Allee, wrote us the sweetest letter apologizing for being ill for our wedding, and ended up with "always be sweethearts." Uncle Shag would shake his big head and say, "Women! You can't live with 'em and you can't live without 'em!" Uncle Sam's favorite, that we have used a lot, was "Never go to bed mad!"

My father used to spout off in public, "A woman, a dog, and a walnut tree: the more you beat 'em, the better they be!" But then he took me off to the side before my wedding and told me seriously, "Son, the way to handle a woman is to find out what she wants to do—and then make her do it!" That's a parable there, and is probably in the Bible someplace or ought to be if it isn't.

The one piece of advice I have probably appreciated most over the years though, came from my wife's Aunt Florrie. It was delivered the week-end of one of our first disagreements, and hunting was the reason.

Like most outdoorsy grooms-to-be, I had quickly tired of the bridal shower/ party circuit, and, when the opportunity for a wild hog hunt on Woodstock Island presented itself, I grabbed hold. Informing my fiancé was another matter, though. That was the weekend of another shower.

19

"Well, durn, there's been one every weekend! Missing one won't hurt me; you're the one they're honoring. And besides, all our ushers and groomsmen are gonna go, too!"

Her solution to that statement was the suggestion that all the groomsmen and ushers could come to the shower. This was received with something less than wild enthusiasm by the male segment of our wedding party, except for one fraternity brother who had his eye on a bridesmaid with long brown hair.

The upshot was that I went wild hog hunting that week-end, and the bride-to-be, alone at her shower, was obviously peeved at her absentee partner. Observing this brewing storm and knowing the reason, Aunt Florrie took her aside during the shower.

"Honey, lemme tell you somethin,'" the elderly lady instructed. "If a man's a man, and he's worth having, he's gonna chase somethin'. It might be whiskey; it might be gamblin'; it might be women; it might be money; it might be huntin' and fishin'. But he's gonna chase somethin'! Just be glad your man likes to hunt and fish, 'cause then you *know* where he is and what he's doin'!"

With this advice in mind, we have since formulated a policy that we have strictly adhered to during twenty-plus years of marriage and hunting. It works like this: since most of my hunting is done several hours away from home, thereby involving several days each trip, I try to let Betsy know as far in advance as I can when I want to go where. Then, after checking her schedule, if she finds there's an event going on during that time she wants me to be back for, she tells me and I'm back for it. The key is that I know she won't ask me to come back (or not go) for something that she doesn't really care about, and she knows that I don't mind missing some hunting for something she considers important.

One of the benefits of this type consideration for each other is that Betsy so sensed the enjoyment I get out of hunting that she became interested in it herself and now hunts with me several times a year. She even owns the only perfect record I know of on deer: she's killed three bucks, has never had to shoot one twice and has never missed! Nor has she let me forget it!

(Let me interject a word of warning to husbands here: if you invite your wife to hunt with you, and if you have access to a cabin in the bondocks, you should know that wives approach these camps with a different standard of cleanliness. She will walk into a hunting cabin considered spotless by any of the male occupants who think about such things, and exclaim: "My lands! When was this place last cleaned?"

Do not take offense. It's just a rule of nature. Simply change your schedule to pick up the little woman in the middle of the afternoon, deposit her at the cabin for her inevitable observation, and depart for the woods yourself for those last few hours of daylight. Just be sure to admire the condition of the cabin quite vocally when you return.)

Back to the original subject. I have several friends who have split the blanket because they couldn't make a lasting arrangement with their wives involving hunting. Several of these were men who had enjoyed hunting for fifteen or twenty years before marrying girls who knew at the time of their marriage that their grooms loved hunting. On the other hand, I've seen marriages break up because the men paid more attention to their hunting than their families. I've quit hunting with a couple of friends whose wives tell them it's okay to go hunting, then give them hell when they arrive home. There's got to be some consideration on both sides and I wish everybody had an Aunt Florrie.

I grew up hunting with one fellow whose wife made him quit after marriage, following several years of major marital disagreements over his going afield. He took up gambling, drinking, and chasing women.

He was last seen somewhere west of Kansas City.

The Hoss Riders

During deer season there roams throughout our Southern woods a breed of men that is set apart. These men are without peers. They are the last remnants of a species that is, as Big Robert used to say, "Rough, tough, and hard to bluff!" These men would have been just as comfortable, maybe even more so, had they been born two hundred years ago. They are called, with all due honor and respect, "Hoss Riders."

While the Hoss Riders are an indispensable part of any well-run successful deer camp, the truest of the true blue of their number usually don't even carry guns. Their dedication is not to the kill, but to the chase. Their pride comes from being able to say, "I put a big ten-point right under that youngest Neill boy's stand. It ain't my fault he missed five times!"

Hoss riders answer to a real need. Our Southern hardwood bottom land forests are liberally sprinkled with wild plum thickets, willow brakes, ironwood sloughs, tornado blowdowns, and canebrakes. Once the season starts, big bucks generally will retreat to these strongholds, venturing out only at night. The solution is to use dogs and Hoss Riders to roust them out. Deer dogs and Hoss Riders go together like grits and red-eye gravy.

Let's pause a minute to consider this canine-equine-human partnership. In the frosty dawn you climb into your tree stand, get comfortable, and load your rifle. As usual, you have forgotten the thermos of coffee you poured just before leaving the cabin; it is probably still in the jeep, but you hate to walk a quarter-mile back for it. You decide to wait until you get cold before taking that hike.

Then from the south comes the ringing bugle of Mr. J's old hunting horn.

25

You know the pack of dogs is about to be "cast." The other Hoss Riders answer with whoops and Rebel yells (the vocal kind, not the bottled kind) to indicate their positions along Duck Slough, over a mile south of your stand. With a north wind blowing, you are in good position, figuring that the deer will probably run into the wind if pushed. Duck Slough, Mill Slough, and three canebrakes lie between you and the drivers. You know you'll see nearly a hundred deer this morning.

The cold and anticipation makes you shiver, just as you hear the pack being turned loose. Two dozen deer dogs a mile south of you join their barks and bays to the yells of the Hoss Riders. Wyatt's highpitched cry indicates he has jumped a good buck, and his pistol cracks three times, not to kill, but to alert the others to his sighting. The dogs strike the smoking scent and break into full voice. The shivers hit you again.

I like to think that when I get to Heaven, the good Lord will let me pick my own pack of dogs for a good run every now and then. It seems like you can never get more than one or two hounds at a time who have those real classic voices, but I have hopes that He'll let me get together all the best-voiced hounds I have known. There'll be a couple of little beagles, like Miss Adventure and her mother, Belle; Chief's old Redbone, Trouble; Peewee's Walker hound, Cicero; the Plott hound we called Bellowin' Buford; and of course, that Black and Tan standard by which all hounds are measured, Jupiter Pluvius.

The chase comes your way, pushed from the east by Dub and his hoarse whoops, and it feels like someone has turned a dozen mice with ice cold feet aloose in your long johns and they are racing from neck to belt and back again. Johnny Mac's shotgun booms thrice, a good sign. One or two might have meant a kill, three's a clean miss. You recognize Bobby Joe's highpitched ram horn sounding from the west and you know you're going to see this deer.

But even if you don't get a shot, this morning has already been worth it.

26

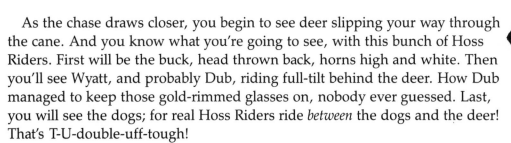

As the chase draws closer, you begin to see deer slipping your way through the cane. And you know what you're going to see, with this bunch of Hoss Riders. First will be the buck, head thrown back, horns high and white. Then you'll see Wyatt, and probably Dub, riding full-tilt behind the deer. How Dub managed to keep those gold-rimmed glasses on, nobody ever guessed. Last, you will see the dogs; for real Hoss Riders ride *between* the dogs and the deer! That's T-U-double-uff-tough!

The story is told of Big B, who was riding close behind a buck one morning on an exceptionally hardheaded horse. Just as Big B leaned to go on the right side of a foot-thick pecan, the horse chose the left. Big B was knocked from the saddle, breaking a couple of ribs. The horse considerately stopped to wait on his dismounted rider. Big B got up, dusted himself off, and retrieved his steed. He mounted painfully, turned the horse and slowly retraced their path for a hundred yards. He then spun the horse around, slammed his spurs into its flanks, and headed full speed for the same tree.

This time, as they neared the tree, Big B gathered both reins in his hands in anticipation of the same tactic by the horse. Sure enough, at the last second, the horse made another move to veer left. Big B jerked the reins with all his might and the horse hit the tree full speed, dead center. Wham!!!

Big B had taken the precaution of removing his feet from the stirrups. When the collision occurred, he bailed off and rolled free. He dusted himself off again, removed saddle and bridle from his former untrusty steed, and walked to the nearest road to catch a ride back to camp. Big B was as surprised as anyone when the horse came staggering into camp half a day later, but it was never any good for riding to the chase again.

Bobby Joe drew a gunshy horse called Tarzan one morning when the camp planned a hunt for a tremendous buck that had been sighted on a small cut-off island. Standers, dogs, and Hoss Riders were barged across the narrow channel, and the standers took up positions while the dogs and riders circled the towhead for the drive through the woods. The dogs struck, and the Hoss Riders spread out, Bobby Joe bringing up the rear. Sure enough, the dogs jumped the big buck along with a bunch of does and smaller bucks. The big deer showed how he had lived to grow such a rack by doubling back and slipping between the riders to escape. Bobby Joe was the only one to spy the buck.

The rider had his rifle today, for this buck was a real trophy. He jerked the gun from the saddle scabbard and spun Tarzan around to give chase. Finally, he was close enough for a shot, but when Tarzan felt the reins drop loose on his neck, he veered to the left in fear of the pending explosion just over his ears. Bobby Joe was unable to get off a shot, and had to resume his chase. Several times he drew close enough, but each time his gunshy mount ruined his aim.

The huge buck got clean away, and Bobby Joe ended up on the far side of the towhead. On the near side, the rest of the riders had finished the drive, and decided to wait on their missing comrade instead of barging back to the island with the standers and dogs. At the edge of the trees they gathered to pass around a bottle of firewater to warm themselves. As the bottle made the rounds, the Head Rider allowed his horse to lead the others in plodding down the sandbar to the edge of the water, where the horses all drank their fill. The Head Rider opined that it was "too deep to cross here," but that there was a shallower ford a couple hundred yards upstream. They all walked their mounts along the water's edge to the designated spot, crossed the narrow stream in stirrup-deep water, then ambled back along the edge until someone pulled another bottle out of a saddlebag. The spot where they paused was right straight across the stream from where their tracks led down the sandbar to the water.

Their bottle was still half-full when Bobby Joe and the Tarzan horse burst out of the trees on the towhead. The unlucky hunter was furious at his mount for making him miss the buck, and was determined to make it pay. Seeing the tracks in the sand that seemingly led straight to where the other riders were waiting, Bobby Joe laid the spurs to Tarzan, gave a Rebel yell, and galloped lickety-split down the sandbar to join his companions, who probably should have yelled a warning, but instead merely watched with mounting anticipation.

Bobby Joe sensed that Tarzan intended to slow at the water's edge, but slowing down was not included in his plans. As they neared the stream, Bobby Joe set his heels to spur his steed while at the same moment reaching to jerk his rifle out of the scabbard by Tarzan's foreleg so the weapon wouldn't be drenched by their crossing.

He had left the safety off.

As the Hoss Rider gripped the gun and started his spur jab, somehow the rifle went off, scaring the pure-D hell out of everybody concerned. The spurring was twice as violent as had been intended and this action, plus the tremendous explosion in the vicinity of his right foreleg, stimulated Tarzan to heights no one present had known horses could attain. Up, up, and away flew the gallant steed with the stunned rider.

What goes up must come down.

Tarzan's descent was just as spectacular. There was a titanic splash that drenched a couple of the onlookers as the horse and rider plunged into the stream. Then only a white hat and ripples remained. The Hoss Rider holding the bottle muttered "Damn!" and took a swig. As the whiskey passed to the next in line, Tarzan and Bobby Joe surged back to the surface, the horse swimming vigorously for the bank. The drenched rider was merely hanging on, obviously having decided his mount did not require as much help swimming as it did jumping.

29

They made dry ground, Bobby Joe stealing a surreptitious glance down and to the right, "just to see if the horse still had four legs," as he later said. Without a word being spoken, the dripping pair plodded up to the awed assemblage, where one of the riders respectfully offered Bobby Joe a drink. Still in silence, he took a long pull at the bottle, handed it back, and wiped his mouth with a sopping sleeve. The bottle made the rounds of the taciturn group back to Bobby Joe, who killed it. The Head Rider mutely wheeled his horse and started for camp at a trot.

They were halfway to camp when the first word was spoken. The Head Rider suddenly reined up, pulled a fresh bottle from his saddle bag, broke the seal, threw the cap away, and took a swig. Leaning forward, he offered the bottle to Bobby Joe and addressed him admiringly, "Son, I'll say one thing: you sure as hell know how to make a horse take the water!"

This same group of Hoss Riders were the main characters in an action that almost ended in a real tragedy. But before we go into that, let me explain something.

The reader must understand that I am not condoning the consumption of firewater in conjunction with the use of firearms. In the preceding story, you will note that the bottle appeared after the hunt was over. There are exceptions, however. Since the Hoss Riders usually don't carry guns, and since they gallop at a breakneck pace through thickets and canebrakes in frigid weather without benefit of cab or windshield, most knowledgeable hunters recognize the need for an occasional warming stimulant when the rider is unarmed. Heck, some of us who are teetotalers would *have* to take a drink if we rode behind a Hoss Rider all morning. Speaking personally, you'd near 'bout have to pour some firewater down me to even get me *on* a horse.

Anyway, I ain't a judge; I'm just a storyteller.

30

Billy Bob had not seen a buck all morning, and he had overheard one of the Hoss Riders at breakfast talking about a late morning drive through the willow brake before they came in for lunch. He left his stand, walked to his truck, and drove down close to the willows. Loading his rifle, he eased through the trees to a small clearing and seated himself on a stump. Sure enough, his hunch was right, for he soon heard the riders' yells, and then almost immediately a small five-point buck trotted into view.

The hunter downed the deer with a neck shot, leaned his rifle on the stump, drew his knife, and walked over to field dress his kill. He had just stooped down when a magnificent buck burst into the clearing. Billy Bob's rifle was fifteen feet away, but he had a nine millimeter pistol on his hip with which to administer any needed coup-de-gras. Now he drew the pistol and proceeded to miss the racing deer three times. He was still staring after the buck when Leroy rode into the clearing.

"Wha'cha got?"

"Got a li'l ole five point; but I just missed a real ole mossyhorn!" Billy Bob, still holding the pistol, indicated that the buck had a spread approaching at least fifty inches. He proceeded to show Leroy how he had shot at the bounding buck. Shaking and jabbering excitedly about the antlered monster, he went to put the pistol back in the holster.

"Blam!" a shot exploded nearby.

Both men froze for a second, then Leroy looked around to see who had fired so close by. Seeing no one, he turned back to Billy Bob, who was standing still as a statue. "Who was that?" Leroy wondered out loud.

Billy Bob spoke carefully. "Leroy, I think I've shot my rear off."

Leroy blinked at the motionless hunter, unbelieving. "Aw, naw you ain't, fella."

31

"I really think I did, sho'nuff. Git down and come look." Billy Bob had still not moved.

Leroy decided to humor him, and swung down off his mount, a little unsteady on his feet. He stepped behind Billy Bob and carefully lifted the hunter's shirttail. There, just above the belt where the holster was, appeared a blue-rimmed hole from which blood was beginning to seep. Leroy was aghast. "Oh my God, Billy Bob! You've gutshot yourself!"

That was all the injured man needed. His eyes rolled back in his head and he fainted dead away. The second Hoss Rider on the scene was greeted by the sight of Leroy holding Billy Bob off the ground by his shirt front and slapping the unconscious man back and forth on the face. "Billy Bob, wake up! Billy Bob, don't die!" he was pleading.

Johnny Mac pulled the tearful Leroy off before any permanent damage was done, and hollered up the rest of the riders. It was obvious they had to get the victim to a hospital right away. The best course of action seemed to be to drape Billy Bob face-down across Johnny Mac's horse and pack him out to his truck. Since the boat landing was between the willow brake and camp, they decided to carry him straight to the landing, cross the river, and head to the hospital emergency room.

Billy Bob had regained consciousness by the time he was placed on the horse, and he was in considerable pain. Leroy swung himself into the saddle, still weeping, and grabbed the reins of Johnny Mac's horse. Johnny Mac walked beside his horse's moaning burden, but he was unable to keep up the pace the concerned Leroy had set. He yelled, but too late.

Leroy led the horse between two trees about three feet apart, scraping Billy Bob off the saddle and tumbling him to the ground.

The unfortunate hunter screamed, and Leroy, again aghast, hurriedly dismounted to help. The whites of Billy Bob's eyes were showing, and Leroy obviously thought he had finished his friend off. He burst into tears again and jerked the wounded man's head and shoulders off the ground by the collar. The slaps sounded like gunshots. "Don't die, Billy Bob! Please don't die!" the sobbing rider pleaded.

Johnny Mac and the other riders rescued the now-revived Billy Bob from Leroy's first aid, and managed to get him back on the horse. This time, Johnny Mac assumed the reins and they all made it to the truck without mishap. They used a couple of saddles and blankets to make the wounded man as comfortable as possible laying face down in the back of the four wheel drive pickup. Before anyone could stop him, the anxious Leroy slid in under the steering wheel and cranked the truck. The rest of the riders piled in, leaving one man to lead all the horses back to camp. Leroy drove at breakneck speed for the landing. Haste was his main consideration, not the comfort of Billy Bob or the riders trying to hold him in and hang on at the same time.

Everyone but Leroy was almost in shock by the time they reached the boats, though they all later agreed that he had made the drive in record time. Billy Bob remained conscious as he was taken from the truck and deposited in a boat, but he was obviously hurting badly. Then just as Leroy grabbed the outboard motor pull-cord, Johnny Mac had a sudden thought. "Hey, has anybody got a key to a car on the other side?"

They stopped and searched, even in Billy Bob's pockets. There was not a key among them.

"Billy Bob, we're gonna have to put you back in the truck and drive to camp. Nobody's got a car key," Johnny spoke apprehensively, for he now feared the delay could mean life or death for the wounded man. His fears were apparently well-grounded, for sure enough, Billy Bob's eyes walled back in his head, and he started to faint away again. Leroy jumped to his feet in the boat, grabbed his familiar hold on his friend's shirt front and drew his hand back to administer more first aid.

That's when the rest of the Hoss Riders knew the victim was going to make it. From some untapped reservoir, he mustered the strength to focus again and pointed his finger in Leroy's surprised face. His voice was almost a roar.

"Dammit, Leroy! DON'T YOU HIT ME AGAIN!"

Harlow's Catch

Reflective Memories

Oak Ridge White Tails

Home Place Covey

Brent's Dog

Black River Deer

Gray Ghosts

Incoming Flight

Back Water Refuge

Timberline Mallards

Bay Lake Squealers

Decoy and Apples

Training
Your Pets

We're not going to be exhaustive here, but most of us have pets around the house and need some basic tips on breaking bad habits and promoting good habits. We're all familiar with the old technique that involves rubbing a puppy's or kitty's nose in the puddle where they wet the floor. Having come from a rural family that raised innumerable pets, I had this routine so ingrained into my character that my horrified wife stopped me just before I used it on our first infant. This actually worked to my advantage, for she refused after that to allow me to change diapers without adequate supervision.

Of course, by the time our third arrived, I had to stop her from house-breaking the child in this manner. By that time, she had seen it work on too many puppies and kittens.

After I was old enough to start building a memory, the first dogs we had were a pair of older, accomplished retrievers, a labrador named Black Gal, and a cocker spaniel called Rusty. So the first dog I remember helping train was a young lab of Uncle Sam's named Spot. It was summertime, and my uncle worked every morning and afternoon teaching Spot to retrieve. He used a fist-sized green rubber ball for every lesson.

Spot was one of those really enthusiastic retrievers, who worshipped his master and would do anything to please him. Whenever Uncle Sam was outside, Spot would beg him to throw the green ball. Sometimes Uncle Sam would chunk it clean over the house, and though it might take Spot a half hour to find the green ball in the green bushes, the lab would finally show up on the back porch with the ball.

Uncle Sam also had a big garden close to the house, where he planted everything from peas and roastin' ears to cantalopes and watermelons. That summer he harvested less of some crops than usual.

One morning the back porch was literally covered with fist-sized green balls, courtesy of a proud, tail-wagging Spot. The watermelons and cantalopes from every garden within half a mile had been carefully sorted by the lab, who was now ready to play retrieve, in spite of having obviously been up half the night. Uncle Sam blew his stack, but his remonstrations were in vain. He had trained Spot too well. For the rest of the summer the lab endured the whippings but never understood the reason his master had turned against him. He dutifully brought home every fist-sized green ball he could find, including watermelons, cantalopes, green tomatoes, bell peppers, and even maypops. Uncle Sam finally gave Spot away to a hunter who lived in town.

We lived in a small town for several years, and therefore experienced the perpetual scourge of the neighborhood, the garbage can turner-over. One year the culprit was a huge German Shepherd who became so bold that he would stand his ground and snarl should you attempt to drive him off before he had finished his inspection of the scattered contents.

One evening I brought home from the farm a small electric fence converter, a device that plugged into the house current and had long wire leads that, when attached to the fence wire, delivered a strong, but not fatal, shock. That evening I hosed down the ground around the garbage can, deposited a couple of delectable soup bones on top of the rest of the garbage, and clipped the wire leads to the handles of the can. I then settled myself into a chair on the back porch to await results. Soon the shepherd appeared on his evening rounds.

Male dogs, once they reach puberty, practice an ancient ritual known to those of us in the trade as "marking the spot." This seems to be a territorial rite and involves the raising of the hind leg to mark fireplugs, light poles, trees, bushes, and most anything else that will hold still. Even garbage cans.

Before the dog touched the electrified can, he advanced upon it with an arrogant expression on his muzzle, "heisted" his leg, and proceeded to mark this can as his very own. It was obviously a shocking experience. As the scientific minded know, most liquids are excellent conductors of electricity, and this dog's marking fluid was certainly first-class in that respect.

His problem was stopping the flow from a full bladder. Every muscle in his body seemed paralyzed except his bladder and his howler. He stood shivering violently with upraised leg, emitting a high-pitched howl, unable to break his flowing connection with the electricity. Finally, mercifully, I pulled the plug.

The shepherd collapsed with a long drawn-out wail into his own puddle. His body contorted with convulsions, his eyes rolled wildly, slobber drooled with moans from his lips. I thought maybe I had gone too far. But then in his pitiful writhing, his tail came into contact with the can, and I remembered how much garbage I had picked up behind this dog.

I plugged the cord into the socket once again. With a full-throated bellow, the German Shepherd erupted to his feet and tore out for the alley. He hit the fence full-speed twice before he found the gate.

He was never known to mess with a garbage can again. In fact, from that day forward, he squatted in the middle of open yards to mark his spots.

While we're discussing helping pets break bad habits, I am reminded of another dog-and-garbage show. My three kids and I were just entering the front yard from a next-door visit when we heard the clatter of an overturning garbage can behind the house. I had the troops and weapons at hand. We had been remodeling, and several pieces of half-inch iron pipe were lying by the front steps. We each armed ourselves with one and ran on tiptoes around the corner of the house to chastise the offending cur. As we silently rounded the house, we saw the can, which for once had been empty, lying on its side with a medium-sized black and white dog all the way up in it. Inspiration struck.

Grabbing the metal can by the bottom, I quickly stood it upside down with the surprised hound inside. I sat on the can while my tribe danced around it with enthusiasm, banging on the can with the pieces of pipe and whooping their war cries. The prisoner joined in with frantic howls for the first few minutes, but these soon subsided to moans, and his initial surges for freedom ceased altogether. Finally, I called off my tiring beaters and gently lifted the can. We expected our prisoner to make a mad dash for the alley, but he just lay there with eyes tightly closed. A yell failed to disturb him—seemed like he had been struck deaf. It took a few kicks to start him on his way, staggering drunkenly. Never saw him at a garbage can again.

All of us are familiar with the car-chasing dog, but those of us with hunting dogs have different chasing problems. A retriever, for instance, is supposed to remain staunch at your side at the shot, mark the bird, and retrieve only on command. I had a friend who bought a large labrador that was only partially trained right before dove season. Dick had always used cocker spaniels to retrieve, and his technique for training them not to break at the shot was to attach a fifteen-foot leash to the dog's collar and loop the other end around his ankle. After hitting the end of the leash a few times, the little cocker quickly learned to "hold." The first day of dove season Dick brought the leash to teach "hold" to his eighty pound lab.

The very first shot he had was on a pair of doves that flared left and right when he stood to fire. Dick dropped the right bird with the first shot and swung left for the classy double. He was pulling the trigger on a northbound dove when an eighty-pound southbound golden labrador at full throttle hit the end of the leash attached to his ankle.

This sort of thing is bad enough when you are all by yourself. But the rules of Southern-style dove hunts dictate that a training exhibition like this must happen in the middle of a field of a hundred friends.

Another friend who owned a young bird dog had a different chasing problem. He was hunting a lot in the hills during the years when the deer population was building up and had a young, fast setter that loved to chase deer. Bobby would yell himself hoarse at the departing Sidney, to no avail. One afternoon, though, I was privileged to be present when Sidney swore off chasing deer.

We were advancing toward an old grown-up fence with a deep gully on the other side, when a buck got up from a briar patch in front of Sidney. The setter gave enthusiastic chase. The deer headed for the fence, and with a fantastic bound, cleared both the fence and the fifteen foot wide gully on the other side. The dog, from a lower vantage point, could not see over the fence.

But Sidney was nothing if not a heckuva jumper in his own right. From a full gallop, he launched himself into a magnificent leap to clear the old fence. He succeeded beyond his wildest expectation and disappeared from our sight. As Bobby later observed, "Sid, you're a great jumper, but you've got a lot to learn about landing!"

Fortunately, the gully was only about ten feet deep, but that was still ten more feet than Sidney had planned on. Also, fortunately, it was only a short walk back to the truck, with me carrying the guns and Bobby carrying Sid. The setter was sore and bruised and one leg seemed either sprained or dislocated, but he was hunting again in a couple of weeks.

Quail only, though. You couldn't pay him to chase a deer.

Fire and Ice

The two hunters had to break ice as they shoved the boat into the lake in the predawn blackness. Big Robert, of course, was a veteran, but this was George's first duck hunt. He settled himself gingerly on the middle seat as his host affixed the old motor to the transom and filled it with gas. Big Robert cussed briefly as his numbed fingers fumbled the gas can cap and it dropped down amongst the decoys piled in the bottom of the boat. "Heck, let's go. We'll find it when it gets light," he said.

The motor cranked after a dozen pulls, and the hunters eased slowly into the open lake. Away from the trees there was enough light for Big Robert to throttle up for the run to the blind, the bow spray freezing on the men's coats and pants. George was shivering noticably by the time they began to pitch out the decoys. "When we get in the blind, we'll break out that thermos of coffee," Big Robert promised.

The blind was a permanent one he and Buddy McMillan had built during summer low water. It consisted of four posts pounded deep into the mud and surrounded by a screen of chicken wire interwoven with switch cane and Johnson grass. The wire screen was not permanently fastened to the posts, but could be moved up or down with the fluctuating water level that rose and fell with the Mississippi River. Having finished placing the decoys, the hunters motored toward the blind, which was entered at one end by pulling the screen open and then closing it behind the boat.

George swung the cane-woven wire door open as per his host's instructions, and Big Robert eased the boat into the blind and killed the outboard. He swung

45

the wire shut behind him and secured it on a spike nailed into the post for that purpose. One thing remained: to conceal the hunters from above, Big Robert pulled the sides of the blind together with a cord across the middle of the boat between him and George. "How 'bout a cup of hot coffee before shootin' light?" he suggested.

The guest accepted the dark brew gratefully. The host delayed pouring his own until he could get his pipe going. He tamped the tobacco in the bowl, reached in his pocket for a big kitchen match, grinned at George, and struck the match with his thumbnail.

The head lit, broke off at the same instant, and flew straight as an arrow down the open spout of the gas can in front of him.

The fumes fired spectacularly, spewing forth and igniting the tinder-dry cane and grass blind wrapped around the boat. Big Robert reacted instantly, grabbing the can by the handle and flinging it over and out of the blind. He jerked the wire door behind him open, grasped the two back foundation posts and gave a mighty shove to propel the boat out of the flaming blind.

The boat went maybe two feet and stopped.

The blind was beginning to burn in earnest now, and Big Robert frantically shoved again. The boat remained fast. The middle cord! He had forgotten it! Leaning forward, he saw by the firelight that the cord was tight across George's knees as the novice crouched on the middle seat, looking wildly for an escape. Big Robert tried to direct George's attention to the restraining rope.

"Jump, George,! Jump!" he bellowed.

Misunderstanding, George looked around him at the dark icy waters and considered them against the burning blind. He sat decisively down on the boat seat and folded his arms across his chest.

"I will NOT!" he declared.

46

Big Robert did manage to get his knife out and slice the cord before his guest was too badly singed. George went home and ordered some golf clubs.

The host's pipe was never found. Big Robert switched to cigarettes and lighters.

Now, this was a case in which the hunter felt he had a choice as to whether to get wet or not. Generally, a duck hunter never has a chance to make such a choice. One second he's dry, the next he's floundering in freezing water over his waders or boot-tops. Yet my hunting partner and I were to some extent offered a choice once.

We were wading across a flooded bean field in water a little over waist deep. This was during a time when I was nursing a bad knee, so my balance was kind of tentative, and got less so when I stepped into a water furrow with my good leg.

I felt myself slowly tipping over, but there was still one chance. My comrade was just about an arm's length away. I reached out to him just as he realized my predicament. Just a grip to steady my balance was all I needed at this point.

Still seemingly in slow motion, my companion—this stalwart youth, this bone of my bone, flesh of my flesh, this strong young lad of ten or eleven winters—assessed my rapidly deteriorating situation and took one step *backwards!*

The first ducking was rather tentative; there was an instinctive resilience in the bad leg that enabled me to rise above the water with my feet still under me. It was the second time under that really did the soaking. Jamming my gun butt into the mud, I finally managed to regain my footing. I cast a scathing look at my son, but before I could launch my tirade, he grinned.

"Daddy, you sure did look funny," he noted. "You went 'Ah-hooomp!' just before you went under!" He puffed out his cheeks in imitation.

47

I know your question before you ask it. No, the opportunity for revenge has not yet arisen. I am still biding my time.

There's a friend from deer camp who is also still awaiting revenge on a couple of his cabin mates. The latter two had gone after ducks instead of deer one afternoon and had found a flooding cypress slough teeming with mallards. As is so often the case in flooded woods, they needed little concealment. The water was about three feet deep at the edge of the slough, but they found two huge stumps, sawn off years before, that were just above water ten feet apart. They tethered the boat rope to a cottonwood sapling, shoved the boat into the nearby willows, and shot their limits while standing on the stumps. They had pulled the boat back to them, and climbed in to go retrieve their ducks when it occurred to them that the river was rising almost a foot a day.

These opportunities only come along once in a lifetime. I probably would have done the same thing.

The next afternoon they returned to the spot with their unsuspecting companion. Hundreds of ducks flushed from the slough as they approached the now invisible stumps, which had been well marked by the conspirators. Ducks circling above them, they pulled hurriedly up to the spot and announced, "We'll shoot from the bank here, the water's not deep." The hunters at each end of the boat then stepped nimbly out into water a foot deep, and stood on the unseen stumps. "Hurry!" they urged their buddy in the middle.

This trusting soul, eyes on a flight of mallards with their wings cupped, vaulted from the boat.

He's still biding his time, too.

I saw a similar vault by my own brother one time, and it was his own durn fault. The day before, my friend David and I had found the ducks using some old fish ponds about thirty miles from the house. We rounded up a party of

five for the next morning. It was about twenty-five degrees, and the wind was blowing about twenty miles an hour from the northeast. The breeze had been out of the west the day before when David and I had put the blocks out. My brother Beau was running the ten-horse motor, so he and I volunteered to rearrange the decoys after the others got out of the boat.

These fish ponds had been drained and planted to soybeans, but the levees were still intact. To keep his crop from flooding in the growing season, the farmer had dug a four-foot ditch around the edge of the twenty-acre field. Now, the beans had been harvested, and the water from the winter rains was about knee deep in the field part where our decoys were. David and I had warned all the others about the ditch.

In waders, Beau and I quickly rearranged the blocks for the northeast wind and jumped back into the boat to cross the ditch, for it was already shooting light. "Bluebills!" we heard David hiss as the bow of the boat hit the levee. I jumped out with my shotgun and turned crouching, hoping to get in on the action. Beau had the same idea, but had obviously forgotten the ditch.

One gloved hand clutching the transom of the boat was all I could see. This type of concealment had not occurred to me.

The other hunters turned in exasperation as Beau's emerging shout flared the decoying bluebills. As much as I enjoy a good duck hunt, there was only one solution here. "Get in the boat," I ordered my brother as I unloaded my gun and stepped in myself. It was a mile-and-a-half-run back to the trucks. He was turning blue by the time he and I got there.

Luckily, I had on two sets of long johns. As he began to stiffly pull off frozen clothes, I cranked his truck and flipped the heater to wide open. Then, standing in the middle of a gravel road with a chill factor below zero, we stripped down. I toweled him off with my shirt and donated my set of

49

thermals. He took off for home as I redressed and headed for the boat. Seems like bluebills were ten point ducks that year, and the four of us limited out by noon.

Beau declined to return with us the next day. Said he wanted to hunt in comfort in one of the old cypress plank blinds we had built in some flooded woods behind his house. That evening, after another good shoot on the ponds, I called to check on how he'd done. His curt reply was that he had given up duck hunting. It took me several days to work the story out of him.

The four-man roofed blind, built about three feet off the ground in a group of hackberries, had been under water from the recent heavy rains. The water had receded to just below floor level, leaving a thick film of slimy silt on the floor. Beau had waded out to the blind, leaned in to set his shotgun on the bench, gripped the rail, and vaulted in through the opening at the rear of the blind. Beau was a helluva vaulter.

His feet hit the slick floor and never stopped. The hunter did almost a complete somersault in the door of the blind, and plunged backwards head-first into the icy water. To give the boy all the credit we can, he did not sell his shotgun and buy golf clubs. But neither did he duck hunt any more that season.

Just Kickin' Around

There is a time of year for all Southern hunters when you quit specializing and just go out kickin' around. Deer season is over, so you're not deer hunting. Duck season's about over so you're not really going after the ducks and you've hung up decoys and waders. It's too early for turkey season. But rabbits, squirrels, and quail are still in season, and if a couple or three hunters get together and go kickin' down the ditch banks, it's a lot of fun. The mixed bag from these excursions might include a half-dozen quail, a dozen doves, a couple of squirrels, six or eight rabbits, a woodcock, a few snipe, a duck or two, and a racoon. One time we even found a half-dozen bullfrogs in an old boat that had been washed down the canal half filled with mud.

I once accompanied a couple of friends on a kickin'-around hunt and nearly saw a young doctor added to such a mixed bag. Happened thisaway:

The canal was up, and the three of us were walking a grown-up spoil bank, stomping brushtops, grass clumps, briar patches, and small canebrakes for whatever game we could jump. Fred walked next to the canal, Dude on top, and I took the field side. This was Fred's last weekend before the second semester of med school started, and he was therefore the most enthusiastic and the least discriminating. When a pair of wood ducks flushed in the canal, he swung and shot the drake, which splashed down in the canal about fifteen feet out.

Now there was an old road that only I knew about that ran between the canal and the ditchbank at low water level. Every five or six years the drainage commission would send a bulldozer to clear this road, and a dragline would follow later, dredging out the mudbars. This old road was now barely under water, making the canal look about ten feet wider than the deep water actually was.

Fred noted the location of the floating duck, reloaded, and began walking forward again. Dude raised an eyebrow at him. "Ain't you gonna get that duck?"

"Too far out. He'll float in and we can pick him up on the way back."

"Aw, fooey! I'll get him," Dude said scathingly.

Cautiously, he stepped out into the water, which was only ankle-deep on his knee-high rubber boots. He planted both feet and then stepped carefully out again. Only a couple inches deeper. He brought the back foot forward, then slowly tested the depth another long step out. Again, it was only a little over ankle deep. He was now standing about ten feet out from the bank, not knowing he was on the edge of the submerged dragline road. He could almost reach the duck with his gun barrel at arm's length.

Confident now, he took one more long step.

His little orange hat floated, otherwise there would have been nothing to mark his disappearance. Fred and I stood dumbfounded. Suddenly, Dude burst into sight from his chest up. "Whoooff!" he bellowed. Remember, this was late January. Fred and I cheered, relieved.

Dude went back under.

Actually, he said later, he was diving for his shotgun, but to us it looked like he was going down for the second time. We started peeling off clothes to go to the rescue, but we really didn't relish the thought. Fortunately, the retriever reappeared. Holding the shotgun in one hand, its barrel dripping mud, he floundered to the edge of the road he had stepped from and tried to clamber up, but the steep drop-off, the slippery mud, and the temperature made his

54

task impossible. Breathlessly, he extended the mud-plugged gun barrel toward Fred and beseeched him, "gimme a hand!"

The med student took a cautious step out into the shallow water and started to reach for the gun. At the last moment, though, he drew back the hand and pointed rather incredulously at the object of the whole wet exercise. It was a classic remark, and the only thing that saved Fred from instant death as a result of it was that the would-be retriever couldn't get out of the water and the muddy shotgun would have blown apart if fired. But Lordee, it was a classic!

"Get my duck, you dummy!"

How to Retrieve

Enthusiastically

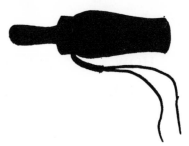

The boy had just entered his teens, and not only was this his first duck hunt, but he was wearing his first set of waders. It was not his first time to wear them, however; he had tried them out the afternoon before in a neighbor's heated swimming pool. The boy had been able to prove to everyone's satisfaction that the new waders did not leak whatsoever up to the point at which water actually ran over the top.

At that point, however, the boy and his audience (father, mother, and neighbor) were able to ascertain that thin boy, copious waders, and slick, slanted-bottomed pools can be a treacherous combination. A two-hundred pound man has very few folds in his waders; put those same waders on a seventy-five pound boy, though, and from the knees up there is little else but folds.

When the first rivulet of water trickled over the wader top just below the boy's thin left shoulder, the weight of the water began to depress the fold, opening the breach to more water, the weight of which depressed the fold even more. The boy tried to back up, but the slick, slanted bottom betrayed him. He had already been on tiptoes, but now the weight of the water in his boots and his sudden need for traction forced the soles of both feet flat to the bottom of the pool.

The levee broke.

The boy, suddenly flatfooted, stood aghast as the water poured into his waders from all sides. His mother later claimed that little swirls appeared around him just like when she pulled the stopper in the bathtub.

59

A decent size swimming pool probably holds fifty thousand gallons of water. While the mother was not aware of the actual capacity of the pool, she quickly determined that all of the water would not fit into the waders. The boy had apparently also reached this conclusion, for his frantic efforts to reverse his slow slide into the deep end now involved thrashing with his arms in perfect execution of a backstroke maneuver that a paid swimming instructor had been unable to make him understand for two previous summers.

The mother's enthusiasm in pointing out her only son's predicament to her husband, who was at the time leaning out to reach for the boy's hand, resulted in the man being propelled into the pool, pipe and all. The neighbor was later heard to claim that the pipe never stopped smoldering. With one long arm, the father snagged the kid by the suspenders, and puffing smoke like an ocean-going tug, dragged his gasping progeny to the shallow end. The mother retrieved her child gratefully, while the drenched, steaming father and the amused neighbor retrieved and emptied the waders.

"In the morning, you wear a belt!" growled the father.

When the two duck hunters departed the house in the star-studded blackness, the waders were strapped securely around the boy's chest by one of the father's old belts. Since the boy had on several more layers of clothes today, the resulting fit was satisfactorily snug, and the father made the observation as they walked down the bank, "Betcha that won't let any water in!"

This was to prove all too correct.

They took their time wading the quarter-mile to the open pocket where the man had left his decoys. The water was a little high on the boy, but there was another cypress about fifty feet from the one the man usually stood against where the bottom rose slightly at the base of the tree, which also had a low crotch where the boy could set his gun. Experimenting, the man found that the boy could take maybe four steps forward before the muddy bottom dropped

60

about a foot. He stood his son against the tree and directed him firmly, "Now, don't you move from here! If you shoot one, I'll get it for you. Understand?"

The boy nodded wide-eyed assent, taking in the treetop-level whistle of wings in the graying dawn. The man grinned approvingly and turned to wade back to his tree. He had gone a little over halfway when, from the corner of his eye, he caught the movement of a pair of widgeons over the blocks. He swung around to point them out to the boy, just in time to see the orange flare of his muzzle blast. The drake dropped like a stone.

The father's roar of "Don't move!" was drowned out by the son's enthusiastic "I'll get him!" The shotgun had luckily ended up in the cypress crotch. Like a sprinter coming out of the starting blocks, the boy covered the four steps of level bottom in two jumps and launched himself on the third bounce as he yelled again, "I'll get him!" In the same breath, the father bellowed once more, "Don't move!"

The water would not have been over the boy's head on the fourth bounce except for one thing: the air trapped in his waders. When the water went over his shoulders, he lost his balance, and the air-filled wader seat greeted the eyes of his horrified parent. Dropping his own gun, the father plowed through the water toward his son for the second time in two days, unmindful of the bow wave he was creating which trickled down his own waders.

The boy's head broke water, and to the father's amazement, there was still a grin on his face. The youth sucked in a breath, and began a disciplined breaststroke . . . toward the dead duck!

Once more the kid drowned out his sire's shout of "Hold still" by his own battle cry: "I'll get him!" He made three series of strokes before the waders won again. The seat propped up and the head went under. The man was gaining, but not rapidly.

Three times more the boy's head broke water. Each time he resumed his

61

enthusiastic progress while crying confidently, "I'll get him!" When the father finally caught him and made as if to return to high ground, the son momentarily fought against such reversal, shipping more water into his exasperated parent's waders. The man lifted the boy into the crotch in the tree and there finally broke the thrashing youth's trance by bellowing, "I'll get the damn duck!" in his face.

The kid perched on the limb, shivering, while his parent retrieved the duck and his own gun. He considerately cautioned, "Be careful, Daddy," when the man lost his balance while lifting the gun barrel from the mud with the toe of his boot. He was lovingly admiring the widgeon when his father declared they had to go back home and dry out. He looked up wonderingly.

"But, Daddy, we've only shot once!"

Ah, youth.

Dissertation on Beating Russ

It was dark enough that my forty-two-year-old eyes could no longer distinguish objects over about thirty yards. I had not seen or heard a turkey all afternoon. With a sigh, I pushed to my feet and picked up my cushion. "Okay, Turkeys," I muttered, "you had your chance." I shouldered my gun and started back down the draw toward the road. The blind was less than a hundred yards behind me when a shot boomed.

By quickening my pace, I arrived at the hogback while the jake was still flopping in front of my fifteen year old son. It was his first wild turkey. Naturally he had heard my hustling approach, and as I puffed up the hogback to him, he did a strange thing. He calmly turned and stuck out his hand to me. "Congratulations!" he said.

That was supposed to be *my* line. It was *his* first turkey. "For what?" I panted, shaking his hand.

He smiled solemnly. "That's the first time you ever beat Russ to one of my shots!"

"But he's not even on the Island this weekend," I protested, puzzled.

The kid stooped to hoist the young gobbler by his legs. "That's probably the only reason you beat him," he stated.

Then he grinned and whooped, and I whooped and slapped him on the back and the "mirating" and storytelling started. But later I began to think on his statement about our old friend whom I had hunted with since years before this boy had even been born.

There is a whole group of men who have raised this boy. He just had the good luck to be the first-born son to friends who had hunted together for years. When he was old enough to begin accompanying me on hunting camp, he was the only youngster in the cabin, and I was a little worried about his reception by my companions. I shouldn't have been.

The first night of deer season, there is usually a matches-for-ante poker game for a couple of hours after supper. It was the first poker game the boy had ever seen, and he observed with interest from first one knee and then another. He was a quick learner.

The second night, the six-year-old busied himself after supper with card table, chairs, cards, and piles of matches. When he was satisfied with his efforts, he called his elders into the room. "We're playing cards," he announced importantly, and began dealing.

If you have never played "Go Fishing" for matchsticks on deer camp, you have missed a treat. Sample conversation:

"Uncle Dude, gimme all your . . . jacks!"

"Dadgummit, kid, you musta peeked!"

"Okay, . . . Uncle Russ. Gimme all your aces."

"Nah, na, na, na, na,! Go Fishin'!"

Not all of us grownups understood the betting system the kid had figured out, but he won consistently for three years. When we taught him to play poker, it was to try to recoup our losses.

I think what I'm trying to tell you here is that a group of friends who had hunted together for years accepted this boy not as a youngster, but as a younger friend. There is a difference. Nobody pampered him, but neither did they talk down to him. He was expected to do his share of the camp chores, but not just kid chores. Russ would bring a special brand of smoked sausage every year, and the boy would slice these links and grill them for our hors d'oeuvres before the steaks were put on. He was allowed to relate his day's

66

adventures on deer stands or in turkey blinds just like the rest of us, and while he wasn't permitted to dominate the conversation, most of the older men seemed to enjoy reliving their own youth by seeing things anew that they may have become jaded to.

At the age of nine, this boy got his first shot at a buck. I was in the tree stand with him, and he was using a 30-30 Winchester that his Uncle Dude had given him. A small eight-point with a half-dozen does had just been jumped by the dogs, and they crossed our clearing forty yards out in single file, the buck last.

All my targeting discussions with the boy had been to the effect that a buck standing still or walking close could be shot in the neck, but a running, or over-forty-yard deer, should involve a chest shot. The boy had practiced faithfully with the little gun and had plenty of confidence in his ability to hit what he was shooting at. Too much, really.

The youngster swung with the speeding buck, and just as I was saying, "If you're gonna shoot" he shot. The deer seemed to stumble momentarily, and the boy yelled "I got him!" I had to grab him to keep him from bailing out of the fifteen-foot-high stand. The buck disappeared into the draw.

"I got 'im, Daddy! I know I got 'im!" Nothing like confidence: the kid had not even levered another shell in.

"Well, let's go see if we can find blood," I said, and began to climb down from the stand. Before I reached the ground, a familiar whistle came from the paw-paw thicket down the ridge. I answered, indicating that the coast was clear.

"Uncle Russ! I got 'im!" the boy shouted.

"Great! Can I see him?"

"He went right over here. I got 'im in the neck!"

Russ and I exchanged glances, mine startled, his questioning. Neck-shot deer are not known for running off. "Where'd you shoot him?" I demanded.

"In the neck," the boy insisted. "I know you said to shoot him in the chest, but he was so close!"

All this conversation took place at a fast trot toward the edge of the draw. It had rained the night before and the herd's tracks were clearly visible. Just over the lip of the draw, Russ pointed to two drops of blood.

"I told you! I told you I got 'im!" The boy was ecstatic.

That was it. For an hour we searched in vain for more blood. For another hour we kicked every brush top for a half mile. The boy sat atop a stump and wept silently when Russ and I finally agreed we would have to give up. The next evening just before dark, Russ killed a small eight-point with a fresh cut across the leading edge of his neck. One-half inch further and the boy would have had his first buck. Russ saved him the horns.

The next year I was again in the stand with the boy, who was this time armed with his grandfather's .243. My stand is a homemade iron basket big enough for two that rests on four legs and was secured to a Y-shaped box elder. The Y was just high enough above the stand for a grown man to use as a rest and shoot across the draw. The ten-year-old was not tall enough to even see across the Y. That's where the buck came from.

This was a really good deer. Matter of fact, the kid afterward said the first he heard from me was "Damn! What a nice buck!"

But the deer was suspicious, maybe he scented us. He came to the top of the draw and stood there on the edge of our ridge only fifty yards away, but directly behind the tree from the boy. When it became obvious that the big buck was uneasy, I decided to let the boy try him. Screened by the tree, I silently eased the plastic five-gallon pail I had been using as a stool up next to the box elder. Holding the boy firmly to minimize movement and sound, I then set him atop the bucket. By standing on his tiptoes, he could sight through the Y, just about the time the buck turned back toward the draw.

Once again my "If you're gonna . . .," was interrupted by his shot. The deer bolted.

"I got 'im! I know I got 'im!" the boy yelled. "I had the crosshairs right on his neck!"

I was dubious. "Well, let's go see," I said.

The boy was handing down his gun to me when Russ showed up. Babbling almost incoherently, the youngster made his older friend understand that he had just shot "the bull of the woods."

But there was no blood, no hair, no sign of a hit at all. After half an hour, I decided to recheck my bearings. Instructing the other two that I would direct them from the stand to the exact spot the deer had been standing, I climbed back up the iron ladder. As I leaned through the Y, I suddenly saw the problem. Not three feet from the end of the gun barrel, the little .243 bullet had cut a pencil-sized branch. Sighing, I beckoned the two back to the stand and showed them where the bullet had obviously deflected. Once again, disappointment reigned.

When the deer season came around again, I had decided that the boy was old enough to hunt by himself. I gave him the stand and stationed myself about a quarter-mile south next to a canebrake. About nine o'clock, a shot boomed from the direction of the old iron stand. I headed thataway at a fast walk.

Before I reached the draw I heard voices, and seeing the stand was empty, traced the sounds into a paw-paw thicket seventy-five yards east of the stand. Russ was there with the boy, following the now-familiar routine of looking for blood. The youngster informed me that a buck "bigger than that one last year" had stepped from the paw-paws into a logging road, and then wheeled back into the thicket just as he had shot. "I think I hit him. I was looking when Russ got here right after I shot."

69

We searched fruitlessly for another fifteen minutes, then I told the kid to return to the stand and from there direct me to the place where the buck had stood in the old road. When he was out of hearing, Russ beckoned to me. He pointed with his toe to a small hole.

"Here's where the bullet hit. He missed the deer," my friend spoke softly.

"When did you see that?" I demanded.

"Saw it when I got here," he shrugged.

"You mean we've been hunting for a half-hour for a deer you knew he missed clean?" I was slightly incredulous.

"Listen!" Russ hissed. "You tell him if you want to, but I'll hunt 'til dark before I tell that kid he's missed again!"

Now that's a friend!

The boy finally scored the next year as a stander while Russ helped drive the old willow brake. The buck was a beautiful eight-point with high, white horns. Only problem was, the horns were separate from the buck. I had previously instructed the boy that, when shooting at a running deer in the woods, to swing ahead of the deer to a clearing and to fire when he saw horns coming into the scope. Following this procedure, I always shot deer in the neck.

I was to find, however, that there's a lot of difference between forty-year-old reflexes and thirteen-year-old reflexes. The boy's shot broke both antlers off about an inch below the brow tines, the impact of the 30-06 bullet also shattering the buck's skull. After a search we found both horns, one grooved by the bullet and with a piece of skull attached, the other with nearly a half-inch of antler blown away.

Now, I have never had a head mounted, though I've killed lots of nice deer. My father had always mounted just the antlers and I had followed his practice. But Russ asked me as we loaded the deer, "You gonna mount this for him, aren't you? I know a taxidermist that can fix those horns back right."

"Well, I haven't thought about it. Probably not. I bet it would cost a pretty penny to fix the horns back right." I dismissed the thought as a matter of course.

That night after supper Russ and another friend, Charlie, cornered me with drawn billfolds. "Now, listen, you cheap son-of-a-gun," I was admonished, "that's probably one of the nicest deer that kid will ever kill; and it'll always be his first one. If that head is not mounted, he'll never remember it like he ought to. Now we're prepared to pay for it if you'll just have it done!"

That head hangs on the den wall, with the antlers just like they were in the woods. It is not just a reminder of a nice buck downed by an unusual shot less than a half a minute after being sighted. To both father and son, it will always be a monument to the presence and influence of a friend.

Not even a life-long friend. A two-life-long friend!

Why Mine Is Posted

Probably every hunting magazine in America has a couple of articles a year suggesting methods for hunters to use to gain access to private posted land, usually farmland. Most have at least one more a year decrying the increasing incidence of "Posted" signs and giving valid reasons for their occurrence. In taxing my memory, though, I can't remember reading one written by a farmer.

I am a farmer, and I hunt, too. So maybe I could share some of my thoughts and experiences on this subject and help you understand why my land is posted.

Many articles seem to assign most of the blame to the slob hunter: thoughtless, inconsiderate, loud-mouthed, even downright rude. This type of guy has been a big problem to me through the years, though he is not the major reason for my "Posted" signs. I remember one fellow who was the stereotype of a slob hunter. I was hosting an opening day dove hunt, which was well in progress and attended by about forty friends, in a twenty-five acre field. Procedure was for folks to park their cars down a bean field turnrow across a gravel road from the hunt and be transported to their stands in my pickup. I had just picked up Rex and his gear and was pulling out of the turnrow when a green Volkswagon, horn blowing, roared up in a cloud of dust and skidded to a stop directly in front of my truck. A beefy, red-faced man leaned out the window and bellowed, "I guess this blankety-blank place is posted too!?!!"

I was rather taken aback, but managed to nod, "Yep."

"Well, who the hell do I have to see to hunt on this s.o.b.!!!" he yelled again.

"Me," I said in my same quiet tone.

"Oh!" he gulped; then, as sweetly as a Sunday School teacher, "Reckon you'd have room for one more hunter?"

"Nope." I replied just as sweetly.

Loud and foul-mouthed slob hunters don't have to be male, you may be surprised to hear. I once drove up to a local lady schoolteacher who had helped herself to a limit of squirrels in our woods, her car parked twenty feet from a posted sign. After we had chatted pleasantly about her kill and the number of squirrels she had seen, I explained that, since I enjoyed squirrel hunting, too, but couldn't hunt during the harvest season, I tried to keep folks out until later in the year when I was able to hunt myself. She seemed nice (and was nice-looking to boot) so I added that she would be welcome to call and come back then.

She looked at me with a sudden belligerence in her eyes and voice, "You mean I can't come back tomorrow!?"

"No Ma'am," I replied.

I can't print the name she called me as she stomped to her car, slammed the door, and roared off.

This kind of vocal display is the exception rather than the rule, though. Lots of inconsiderate hunters have nice manners and try to be patient with me. Take the young hunter I heard shooting in the middle of a hundred acre soybean field, for instance. The kid wore camouflage, but I finally saw him stand and shoot. I walked out about a quarter mile into the waist-high beans to where he was crouched on a dove flyway between a water hole and a millet field. A twenty yard square of beans was stomped flat in front of him.

I tried to control my voice. "You tromp down these beans?"

"Yes, sir," he replied politely, still hunkered down watching the sky.

76

"Mind telling me why?" I queried, holding myself in check.

"No, sir," said the youngster, standing patiently, "It's hard to find doves in beans this high, so I'm trying to shoot them so they'll fall in that open space." After a slight pause he looked at me (a little piously, I thought). "I think it's a sin to shoot game and let it go to waste. Don't you, sir?"

Crop damage like this has always been a minor problem, but has picked up in recent years with the increased popularity of four-wheel drives and all terrain vehicles. In my experience though, most of this damage is done as malicious mischief, usually by teen-agers or drunks.

The fact that they have guns doesn't make them hunters. That seems to be secondary to the damage they can do and all the "Posted" signs in the world won't stop them. As far as I am concerned, people like this have taken themselves out of the category of slob hunters and into the classification of outlaws.

The law breaker is one of the main reasons my land is posted. He comes in several different categories, such as trespasser, vandal, poacher, game-hog, spotlighter.

Simple trespassing is the most common. People don't seem to realize that a farmer usually considers his acreage just as much his as they do their own yards. If you were to see a stranger wandering around your back yard, sniffing the flowers, testing the comfort of the lawn furniture, checking the garbage can contents, you would probably call the cops. You would certainly consider it an invasion of your privacy and demand that the fellow explain himself. And it just might turn out that he's a nice guy whom you don't mind having around. Point is, the polite thing to do is to ask first!

If I know the game they are hunting is plentiful enough, I nearly always will accommodate hunters who come early to ask permission. On the other hand, I have made it a rule to ask those who just make themselves at home and start hunting without permission to leave at once. Sometimes this makes for ugly scenes.

When I was in high school, my father heard some shots at a dove roost nearly a mile off the gravel road. It had just rained, so he told me to take the jeep and investigate. I was getting ready for a date that night, so didn't even have hunting clothes on.

As I approached the roost, I saw one man standing in waist-high cotton. The field next to the roost thicket was planted in skip-row; four rows cotton, four rows fallow skip. I drove down one of the skips to the hunter. He was awful looking: unshaven, rough clothes, long greasy hair—I wondered if maybe there had been a prison break.

I stopped some twenty feet from the fellow and left the motor running (both prudent decisions, it turned out). "Mister, you can't hunt here, this land is posted."

He just stood and stared at me.

"This is posted land. You can't hunt here," I explained a little louder.

He gave a short laugh, then raised his own voice, "Hey boys! This kid says we can't hunt here!"

Six more men, all stamped from the same mold, stood up from the cotton, all within thirty yards of me. "Let's show him some manners," the leader said.

Fear makes for wonderful reflexes. I slammed the jeep in reverse and floored it. Only the sloppy footing kept the closest one from catching me. I backed up out of shotgun range and stopped to address them once more. "I'm going back to call the Sheriff," I yelled. "If y'all are still here when I get back, you'll be sorry!"

When my father and I returned, they were nowhere in sight.

I think the most classic case of trespassing and threats I ever heard of

happened to my younger brother, who was in high school at the time. It was the opening weekend of dove season. I had patrolled the field on Saturday and had asked about forty uninvited hunters to leave during the day. Somehow, people can't seem to understand that if you have nearly a hundred invited friends, some from hundreds of miles away, you don't want strangers crowding them and ruining their hunt.

Late in the afternoon, I decided to shoot a while myself. I noticed a couple of hunters walking in from the road, but kept on hunting since it was getting close to sundown.

At our hunts we have made a practice through the years of not going to the field on Sunday until folks have gotten home from church, changed clothes, and had a bite of lunch. About one o'clock on the second day, a bunch of us were sitting on the front porch feeding our faces when two pickups and five cars drove by. As we watched, they turned in the dirt road to the dove field, drove the half-mile to the gate, parked the cars under a willow tree, put all the people in the pickups, and distributed thirty-five hunters around the field in the best spots.

Beau had finished his lunch, so he volunteered to drive up and tell them we planned to hunt there with our own guests, thank you. In about ten minutes he was back, white-faced and shaking with anger. "They told me to go to hell and ran me out of our own field! I need some help!" he sputtered.

When a truckload of us returned to the field and started rounding up uninvited guests, we were completely unprepared for the "head host's" reaction.

He shook his finger in my face and spoke with wrathful indignation. "This is highly embarrassing to me," he exclaimed, "these men are all friends of mine and I've invited them to hunt!"

79

"In my field?" I asked incredulously.

"Well, I hunted in it late yesterday afternoon and no one asked me to leave!" he stated righteously.

He left that day, though.

A farmer hates to have ugly confontations like this for more reasons than the fact that they leave a bad taste in his mouth. Most of us have several hundred thousand dollars worth of equipment too far away from the house to hear somebody tampering with. That's not to mention fences, gates, livestock, irrigation wells and systems, and grain bins scattered across our acreage. Several times a year I experience vandalism or thievery, and I suspect some of it has been disgruntled hunters who have been asked to hunt elsewhere. I know one instance was.

A twenty-five-acre pasture that bounded the woods had a pair of high cypress gates that swung together and were secured with a piece of chain over a spike nail. A fellow who lives down the road had been slipping in to 'coon hunt by driving through the pasture to the edge of the woods. Since I don't hunt 'coons, I hadn't tried to stop him until one Saturday night he left the gate open and I had to spend half of Sunday rounding up cows. The next week I pulled the gates together with a longer piece of heavier chain and padlocked it. That weekend, the cows were out again. The guy had used a chain saw to cut the gates in two at each set of hinges, then loaded the gates in his truck and took them home with him!

I once lost most of the fence posts on one side of this same pasture. I had fallowed the adjoining field, which had grown up to weeds during the busy fall harvest. An early frost dried the vegetation, and one weekend a couple of rabbit hunters set the field on fire to run the rabbits out. We managed to save a tenant house in the field, but the fence posts burned merrily. The two rabbit hunters replaced them, not nearly as merrily.

Speaking now as a hunter even more than as a farmer, the lawbreaker I have really grown to hate is the deer poacher. My neighbor and I have about seven hundred acres of woods and have carefully nurtured a small deer herd for nearly fifteen years. A few years ago we judged that they had reached the point that we could harvest a buck or two. But word got out among the local poachers, and in a month's time, at least twenty-one deer were killed from our herd, most by spotlighters. These outlaws rode three-wheelers and butchered the deer on the spot, taking only the loins and hindquarters. A tough game warden finally stopped them, but no one was ever brought to trial.

One huge buck escaped the massacre. We saw him several times over the next four years and I don't doubt he was Boone and Crockett material. This past winter we decided to hunt the woods again, and though I jumped him once, nobody got a shot at the big buck. Two weeks after the season ended my neighbor found him three-days-dead in a little church yard close by the woods. Gutshot with buckshot, we think by spotlight, this majestic animal had suffered a slow agonizing death.

I was tempted once to kick a former friend of mine who was the cause of my early-season squirrel hunting ban. He obtained permission to hunt and had done so for three weekends before I finally got a chance to go myself. I had a disappointing morning and admitted it when he saw me at church the next day.

"Man, you ain't much squirrel hunter," he bragged. "Why, I got thirty-five just the first morning!"

No wonder I hadn't seen any! And he hasn't seen any more in my woods, either!

Maybe you are thinking by this point that there have been an awful lot of personal pronouns in this: *my* deer herd, *my* woods, *my* squirrels, *my* ditchbanks, etc. Well, according to courthouse records, I do own the land. And unlike a lot of farmers, I try to take care of my game just like my crops. I have resisted the trend to bulldoze every tree in sight, like some of my neighbors. All the fence lines, sloughs, ditchbanks, and tree lines that were here twenty years ago are still here. I've made it a practice each fall when I finish planting wheat to take the fifteen or twenty bushels left over and, instead of taking them back for credit, put them in a sling seeder to sow into the edges of the tree lines and ditchbanks. I do the same thing with both milo and soybeans in the spring. This provides both cover and food for small game like rabbits and quail.

These days farmers get blamed for killing off all the quail with pesticides. I poison my crops when I have to, but I consistently have fifteen or twenty coveys of quail a year because I have preserved their habitat.

Leaving the treelines not only prevents soil erosion and crop damage from spring winds, but provides nesting areas for doves and other birds, as well as a home for squirrels, 'coons, and 'possums. Deer use them for cover and travel.

When we cut firewood from the woods, I take mostly ash and hackberry, with a minimum of oak. This gives me a high percentage of mast trees, pecan and oak, for food for squirrels, deer, and ducks. Parts of these woods are low, and flood in the winter. An old slough that used to drain them has been dammed up by beavers which I leave alone to do their business. Some of the trees have died along this slough, of course, but water stays there even in summer and nobody around raises more wood ducks than I do. Plus, in the spring and summer, we enjoy many a frogleg from this and other sloughs.

Every farmer has to fallow some land, and it is easy to plant a patch here and there of millet, milo, rice, sunflowers, corn, or soybeans for what the government calls a "wildlife food plot." I plant some in low areas, then close up a water furrow or so to flood for ducks in the winter. Patches on higher ground

82

are great for dove shoots. Deer will view a few acres of sunflowers next to the woods as a delicatessen, walking down the rows and taking small bites out of the plate-sized heads that hang down to shoulder height.

Other wildlife benefits from all this besides game. There are seven beaver dams on the small canal that winds through my place. In addition to the beavers, muskrat, and nutria common here, I also see otter and mink. Foxes and bobcats provide predator calling sport, and we get an occasional wolf. Itinerant panthers come through every couple of years, believe it or not. One of my tractor drivers found a set of tracks recently that mystified us but we believe were made by a bear.

All this leads up to what one of my tenants would call my "most mainest" reason for posting my place. It's simply that I hunt, too. My brother lives out here, and he hunts, as well as my son. The three of us and our friends can harvest almost as much game as can safely be taken off our acreage each year, and as any farmer knows, you have to save seed for next year. So when a hunting farmer turns you down, it may be quite simply that he's taking care of what he considers a crop.

Let me give a few important tips for gaining permission to hunt, from a farmer's viewpoint. First, as mentioned before, always ask a day or so ahead, if possible. And it really helps if you've taken the time and trouble to make a few visits and become friends. (It's been said down here that nobody has more friends than a farmer with a field full of doves on opening day. But there are degrees of friendship.)

Speaking of opening day, if you know a farmer is hosting a hunt, bear in mind that he probably already has a full quota of invited guests. Don't put him on the spot by calling the day before and asking for an "invite." But do keep the place in mind for the next weekend. After the out-of-town guests have gone, he will usually welcome extra hunters to keep the doves flying. When you come to a large hunt, bring a big water cooler, or an ice chest full of drinks, and volunteer to make one of the rounds for your host. He will definitely appreciate it. A farmer seldom gets to hunt if he's the host unless someone does this.

Also, if you are invited to a hunt, don't invite your own buddies. If I plan a hunt for, say, seventy-five guns, and one fourth of them bring an extra, then I've got a crowded, possibly unsafe field. You may know brother-in-law is a careful hunter, but I don't. And if he peppers one of my friends, the guest list may be short your name next time.

When you get permission to hunt a place, one of the worst things to do is to show up with a couple of friends, and not just from the standpoint of crowding, either. From experience, let me tell you what happens: Tom gets permission to hunt for himself, then brings Dick for company. The next week Tom can't come, but Dick brings Harry. If I have decided there are enough squirrels for ten outsiders to hunt and they all do this, by the end of the season I've got thirty extra hunters. And they all want to come back next year, so I've got to make somebody mad by turning them down. Easier to refuse everybody.

If the farmer has time, get him to make you a sketch of his place and mark where it's okay for you to hunt and where it's not. Keep your distance from barns and houses, grain bins and irrigation systems. If you observe other hunters breaking these rules, always be sure you inform the landowner. Not only will you escape the possible blame for something, but he will probably welcome you back if he knows you are looking out for his interests.

Be sure to ask the farmer what game he may not want you to shoot. I will always instruct visiting hunters to leave quail and deer alone, but in case your host forgets, it's better to know any such restrictions up front. Conversely, you might ask if there are any animals besides those you're hunting that he wants shot. A farmer with livestock might want armadillos killed, for instance. A corn

84

farmer might like to see some 'coons taken out. A man who hunts his own quail would welcome your taking care of almost any predator, especially wild housecats.

Always make it a practice to either stop by after the hunt, or if that's not convenient, to call and thank your host. If you've been lucky, offer him some of your bag—cleaned, or at least, field dressed. Be sure to inform him of what you've killed, where you killed it, and anything out of the ordinary you have observed on his acreage.

Above all, observe the final instructions my father used to give visiting hunters: take care of it like it was yours! Don't litter, don't be careless with fire or shots, don't rut up turnrows, don't injure crops, livestock, or trees, don't break game laws, and don't tolerate this type behavior from other hunters you encounter. Consider yourself just as much a guest on the farmer's land as you would in his home, and conduct yourself accordingly. And maybe, for your purposes, the ultimate reward will be yours the next year.

Maybe he will call you and ask, "Would you like to hunt on my place again this year?"

Please, Mr. Warden

While I consider myself to be a law-abiding citizen and a staunch supporter of game laws, I would be lying if I said that the sudden appearance of a warden didn't make me a little nervous. I think that may result not so much from past sins, but from hosting so many plantation dove hunts over the years. When you have a large group of people together for an activity that most of them consider to be more social than hunting, you increase the chances that someone may have overlooked the letter of the law with no evil intent. Samples: "Well, heck. I thought licenses went from January through December"; "That extra dove is Tom's. It fell on my side of the pond and I picked it up for him"; "Shucks! I unplugged my gun last deer season and this is the first time I've picked it up since then"; and "I thought it was from sunrise until a half hour after sunset!"

And of course, there's always the classic from duck season: "Would you believe that mallard hen was flying with a flock of gadwalls?"

So I prefer to think that the presence of a game warden doesn't rattle the chains of ghosts in my own closet, but stirs concern in my heart for the possible sins of others. As a pure-D matter of fact, I have been friends with several wardens and have appreciated their help when poachers and night-shooters descended. Many times we invited wardens to dove hunt with us and made sure everybody knew it ahead of time so we wouldn't have to worry about who was or wasn't legal.

There was one such sincere invitation that saved probably a hundred hunters from citations for shooting over a baited field. On an Opening Day dove shoot,

PLEASE,
MR. WARDEN

Cousin Crawford had a hot fence corner and limited out in jig time. He was standing at my pickup with a cold drink when two wardens drove up to check the field. They introduced themselves and said they'd like to check things out, and one stayed to start on our end while the other one drove to the far side of the field to start there.

Crawford was a gregarious type, a hail-fellow-well-met who never saw a stranger. He forced a cold drink on the warden without twisting his arm too much, and began to haul out his own license, doves, and shells. The warden okayed the license and limit, and was checking the gun when a flock of a dozen doves swooped over the treeline beside us. Crawford pointed urgently, "Take 'em, fella, take 'em!"

The warden reacted instinctively, dropping the first dove like a stone, and feathering a second that I sent the retriever after. The warden grinned proudly as the dog pounced upon the second bird, and Crawford slapped his knee and exclaimed, "Mankind! A double to open the season. You think that gun ain't trained?!!"

"Whatcha mean, gun? That was pure-D shootin' skill!" the warden boasted.

"Luck!" I chimed in as I took the dove from Windy. "That wouldn't happen again in a month of Sundays!"

"Betcha a box of shells he can do it again," Crawford challenged. "I tell y'all, that gun's trained!"

The warden was on the spot now, and tried to give the shotgun back to Crawford while he was still ahead and had bragging rights. "Man, I can't be shootin' out here; I gotta check the field."

Crawford was having none of that. "Aww, you gotta love huntin' to do your job. Now, when's the last time you took half an hour and just enjoyed yourself?"

"Been a while," the warden admitted. He still held the gun.

90

"You can at least shoot till you finish your sodie water," Crawford urged. "I gotta box of shells ridin' on the next pair comes in." My cousin was sincere in feeling sorry for a man who enjoyed the sport but had little time to hunt because of protecting the game. He held his vest out to the warden.

"Well, just until I finish my drink," the warden said, and promptly powdered an incoming pair that cost me a box of shotgun shells. Crawford chortled and punched me. "Go ahead, fella, we're shootin' for free now!" he encouraged his guest.

Ten minutes later, the warden had eight doves when we were interrupted by the fast approach of his partner's pickup. The truck skidded to a stop by us and the driver jumped out. "Hey, we gotta shut this field down and arrest these guys! It's been baited!" Suddenly he took in the warden's vest, gun, and doves. He stopped and gaped.

We later learned that a neighbor on the other side of the treeline had cleaned out a grain bin and piled the wheat up in his pasture for the cattle. Really, none of us had known it. I was just starting to protest when our warden hunter jerked the vest off and thrust it and the gun at Crawford. He glared at us and laid down the law. "You got fifteen minutes! I'll arrest any one in the field after that!"

I don't think he ever believed us.

Ever hear of a fellow volunteering to be checked by a warden? Surprised me, too. We were hunting doves in the long, narrow old pasture the second day of the season when two wardens showed up. It was early, so the shooting was rather slow, and the wardens started up the fence line to make their checks. Suddenly, every hunter's attention was attracted to a booming voice from the ditchbank. The wardens turned.

"Hey!" the long tall hunter yelled, "Wait! Check me!" He came from under a chinaberry tree and strode the seventy-five yards across the open field, continuing his loud harrangue the whole distance.

"I know my rights! I wanna be checked! I've been huntin' for twenty years and I've never seen a live game warden in the field! I thought all you guys did was sit around in air conditioned offices with your feet on the desk or drive around in air conditioned pickups list'nin' to country music! I wanna be checked!"

The game wardens' jaws were clenched as the hunter neared them, still agitating on his theme. "Man, I'm gonna recommend y'all to my congressman! Wait'll my ole daddy hears I saw a coupla live game wardens! Here, look at my license!" he demanded to one of the men. To the other he handed his gun and some shells. "You check my gun, and I'll help y'all count all these doves." He began to pull birds from his vest and pitch them at one warden's feet. "One. Two. Man, I'm sho' glad to see y'all! Three. Ain't much sense in checkin' that next guy. He couldn't hit a bull in the butt with a bass fiddle! Four. Five. . . ."

The warden with the gun put five shells in it. He smiled pleasantly and politely interrupted the boisterous hunter. "Did you see what *I* just did, sir?"

This stopped the monologue. "Naw, wha'd you do?" was the loud query.

"I just put five shells in this gun!" the warden beamed.

The loud one's voice suddenly dropped. "Naw, you didn't!" he declared, incredulous.

The warden just shrugged and started pumping. Sure enough, "One, two, three, four, five," his partner helped him count the shells out loud.

For a moment the hunter stood there open-mouthed. Then, "Put 'em in again!" he demanded suspiciously.

The warden seemed more than happy to oblige. "One, two, three, four, five," he recounted, smirking. Whoops began to sound from the other hunters close enough to realize the loud one had met his waterloo.

92

"But I just picked up that gun from the gunsmith's! *He* musta left the plug out!" was the agonized protest from the hunter. We could tell he had a premonition of what was coming down the road. "What happens now?" he asked meekly.

One of the wardens smiled sweetly as the other pulled out his ticket book with a flourish. "Oh, sir, we give you a little ticket now. Your congressman will be *so* happy to know we're doing our duty!"

I never volunteered like that, but I was sure happy to see a warden show up once. Little Dave and I had taken our high school coach to a pothole we knew about on the River. The water was falling, and we had to run the boat up on the mud bar, slop through two hundred yards of knee deep mud, then wade a quarter mile of flooded woods to reach the hole. All this with guns, shells, and two sacks of decoys. (Guess who got to carry the decoy sacks?) We were some kinda tuckered when we got to the pothole, but the mallards we jumped out of it revived us. Wading in waist-deep water and mud, we arranged our blocks and backed up to a clump of big willows as the sky began to redden in the east. I shivered with cold and excitement at the whisper of wings above us. Dave got out his call and hailed. A flock began circling and answering.

Suddenly, from our left, a shot boomed at the flock above us. The flash from his barrel was still orange as the mallards flared away, unscathed. The pothole wasn't but a hundred yards long, and the fellow was nearly to the other end of it, downwind. He had no decoys, but every flock that stooped to ours would have to come over the man. "Skybuster!" cussed Coach, barely audible.

As the morning brightened, that epithet became louder and louder from Coach. Flock after flock tried to decoy, and each time the skybuster would flare them, but without downing any himself. It became obvious that he was operating only from meaness. Coach yelled at him a couple of times, but the

 93

guy never acknowledged. By eight o'clock, we had only bagged one teal that had slipped in with the wind. As I waded back from retrieving it, I glimpsed a movement of olive green and the glint of a badge back in the trees.

"Warden's back in the willows," I warned my companions in a low voice.

"Well, I wish he'd arrest that son-of-a-gun for skybustin'!" Coach fumed. Dave and I could tell he was having to bite his tongue to keep from cussing in front of us. "We ain't got but one duck, so he might as well come check us."

But the warden remained hidden, and the ducks continued to try to come in, while the skybuster continued his harrassment. Coach was sputtering so bad he couldn't even call. Finally, the guy crippled down a mallard hen that staggered the length of the pothole before falling within ten feet of Coach. Durned if the skybuster didn't wade right out across the middle of the pothole to retrieve her. Bold as brass, he approached through our blocks, flaring ducks all the time, and said, "How 'bout pitchin' me my duck!"

I mean, didn't even say "please"!

The man's tone and demeanor just flew all over Coach. He shoved his gun at me and took two steps away from the tree to pick up the mallard. Then he wound up like a baseball pitcher and flung the hen as hard as he could at the skybuster who was maybe twenty feet away in waist deep water taking another step.

"Here's your damn duck!" Coach roared.

I have never weighed a duck, but I would guess that a good-sized hen mallard might go three or four pounds. By the same token, I have never measured the velocity at which said duck can be thrown by an athletically inclined man. But I can testify for lead-pipe certain that the combination of these two factors can cause a man in waist-deep water to lose his footing and go completely under.

94

The skybuster burst sputtering to the surface, and the first thing he did was check his gun barrel. Fortunately, it was dripping mud, for there is no doubt in my mind that had it been clean, Coach would have died right there. The infuriated skybuster and the irate Coach surged toward each other as Little Dave and I began to consider our options. (Actually, Dave was considering his; I was holding two guns, so I couldn't shoot.)

Suddenly, gunshots boomed twice at such close range that the two would-be combatants were temporarily immobilized. The warden I had seen earlier stepped into view, the smoking pistol in his hand.

" 'Scuse me, fellas, but I need to check your licenses if you got a minute." He holstered the pistol and started to me and Little Dave, the closest to him. He glanced only briefly at ours, and only a little longer at Coach's. The skybuster, though, was another matter.

"Hey, I can't read a thing on this," the warden pronounced, squinting at the dripping piece of paper.

"Reckon you can't. It's all wet!" the man retorted hotly. "That son-of-a . . ."

"No cussin' in front of these kids!" the warden interrupted in a steely voice. "You arguin' with me?"

"Hell, naw! But I'm legal. That son-of-a . . ."

"Fella," the warden hissed grimly, "I ain't warnin' you again about cussin'. That's near 'bout resistin' arrest. I 'spec' I better take you in. I can call to check on this license when we get to the bait shop at the landing. Unload that gun."

The skybuster seemed to want to protest once more, but a glance at the warden's countenance stopped him. Gritting his teeth, he unloaded the gun and started in the direction the warden pointed as the lawman stuffed the wet license in the shirt pocket behind the badge. The skybuster was out of earshot when the warden turned to us.

95

"Now you boys have a good hunt," he grinned.

We let out a sigh of relief as the warden started wading off, but then Coach remembered. "Mr. Warden, you want to give that fella his duck?" he asked meekly, holding up the hen.

The warden considered only a moment before he shook his head and winked. "You better keep that duck. I sure don't want you throwin' it at me!"

The Skunkshooters

The Mississippi was high, a condition we see too seldom during duck season, and cold weather had brought the ducks down. The river had crept up over the sandbars, flooding grass fields and cockleburr flats, and every little slack-water cove you could find was chock-full of mallards. Ducks flushed noisily in the grey dawn as Dude, Vernon, and I motored around behind Montgomery Bar and began to throw out decoys in the flooded weed field between the willows and the bar. Another couple of days of rising river would put the bar plumb under, I noted. It was already cut off from the main island.

Decoys set, I eased the boat up to the grassy bar to let the other two out. I would take the boat a hundred yards upwind, beach it, and throw some branches across it for camouflage, but there was no sense in all of us walking that far, not in waders. Dude started to step out, then suddenly jumped back into Vernon's lap. "Back up! Back up!" he yelled.

The clump of grass I had pulled up to had been the refuge of a full-grown skunk, and he was now business-end to us as my passengers frantically grabbed the paddles to reinforce the slowly backing motor. We moved safely out of his range and I endured the expected abuse about my boat driving, the main thrust of which was that I had known the skunk was there.

"One thing for sure," I opined, noting the nearly flooded bar, "there ain't much place he can go!"

I let them out safely and hid the boat back up the bar, as planned. On my walk back to the blind, I crossed paths with the skunk again, but I had expected to, and gave him plenty of room. My companions had already shot into one flight of ducks before I reached them.

We collected our limits before long, and then stood silently in the waist deep water just watching them work for a while. The wind was beginning to pick up considerably by the time we decided to call it quits. Dude volunteered to walk to the boat with me. "With the wind blowing this hard, we'd better get the blocks up before Vernon gets in the boat," he allowed, and we agreed with him. The two of us began walking into the wind.

We had forgotten the skunk, but when we jumped him again, it was obvious that he was incensed by this third invasion of his territory. He refused to back down and, as a matter of fact, advanced toward us, tail held high. Dude swung his shotgun up, but I grabbed his arm. "Don't shoot! He's upwind of us!"

Backing slowly into the edge of the water, we made way for the peeved skunk. As soon as he was past us, we sloshed back onto the bar. Dude raised his gun again. "He can't get away with that!" he muttered. The polecat was now about twenty yards downwind of us. But he was also thirty yards upwind of our comrade still in the blind. Vernon must have had a premonition, because the thought hit all three of us at the same time.

Dude and I looked at each other and grinned.

Vernon bellowed, "Don't do it! I'll kill you!" And he probably would have had we been in shotgun range. And we probably deserved it.

"Boooom!" our shotguns spoke in unison. The skunk, mortally wounded, released his spray in a visible mist. Our downwind companion's cursing became muffled as he sought the only refuge available from the foul stench.

None of us had any idea just how far a pair of rubber waders would stretch. We two skunk shooters later testified that Vernon disappeared completely into his boots and closed them over his head. Fortunately, the brisk wind had dispersed most of the smell by the time Dude and I began to pick up the decoys.

Several minutes of negotiations were required before we agreed to pick up our fuming comrade. He was quite graphic about his intentions toward us, and only the fact that we were in the boat and he was marooned on a small sandbar with a dead skunk and a rising river quieted him. Grudgingly, he finally admitted that he would probably have done the same thing, and unloaded his shotgun.

But he promised as he stepped into the boat, "By golly, I'll get you skunkshooters back someday!"

Firewater

Having already revealed right up front that some hunters consume alcoholic beverages, I don't guess I'd get in any worse trouble by discussing frankly some of the incidents brought on, not by the consumption, but the overconsumption, of firewater.

Let me say from the start that our cabin for a number of years boasted the best liquor collection on the island. The reason for this was that Big Robert, Beau, and I didn't drink. Well, I'll clarify that in a minute; but the point is that hunters from other cabins who were packing to leave after several days at hunting camp would visit our cabin before leaving. After goodbyes, they would ask, "Say, could I leave this half-fifth of Wild Turkey with y'all? There's no sense in taking it off the island, but if I leave it in my cabin, those guys will drink it!" We kept the leftover liquor for everybody in camp, most of whom promptly forgot that they'd had any left.

When I said we didn't drink, I meant what was called "hard likker." Big Robert was an alcoholic. He quit cold turkey when I was five years old, but I never heard him say, "I *used* to be an alcoholic." His contention was that "the next drink is the one that throws you off the wagon." And he convinced both us boys that the condition was hereditary.

When I was overseas I learned to drink wine, and later liqueurs. The first time I went ashore, I didn't believe the medic's harping on "don't drink the water!" Three days later and ten pounds lighter, I was able to go ashore again. Now my choice of beverages was narrowed to a fifty-cent bottle of what my companions claimed was good wine or a small coke for a buck and a quarter. That same coke was a nickle back on board ship.

According to family legends, an ancestor of mine not only Christianized Scotland, but *named* the land, in honor of a family matriarch. The lady's name was Scota, and she was the daughter of a Pharoah and married to King Milesius of Spain. With that history, could I pay twenty-five-hundred percent for a coke?

Dinna' fret, laddies; I learned to drink wine.

Beau, now, will partake of maybe one beer after a real hot day on the lake. As far as I am concerned, you can pour that stuff back in the horse. I once saw an enthusiastic young hunter dragged from the house because of it and was truly surprised when I saw him alive the next day.

The unnamed young man had been invited on his first (and nearly his last!) Plantation Dove Shoot. He arose early that morning and disdained breakfast in his haste to embark on the several-hour drive, so as not to be late for the noon opening. He arrived at the home where his host had a dining table just groaning with the weight of meats, vegetables, fruits, salads, breads, casseroles, and desserts. (The rule on Plantation Dove Shoots is that everybody brings as much food as possible, and puts it on the table; when the food is gone, the hunt is over.)

Our excited subject ignored his host's urging to eat a good lunch and obtained permission to depart for the dove field a full hour before shooting time, in order to get a good spot. Once there, he unloaded cooler, water jug, gun, vest, and shells at his chosen site, then parked his car on the road and readied himself for hunting. He checked his license twice, his gun plug thrice, and then waited impatiently in the ninety-degree heat for noon. He knew the host's rule was that the beer in the cooler couldn't be broken out until he had finished shooting, but he could smell it and hear it calling him right through the sealed bottles and the closed lid.

On really hot days, the doves sometime don't fly well until after three o'clock. Such was the case this day. The young hunter had only picked up three doves by mid afternoon, so was sunburned and frustrated when suddenly the grey darters began to flock into the field, "thick as bees," as the saying goes. It took three boxes of shells during the next hour to bag his limit, none too soon, for the novice had been out of water for two hours. Gratefully, he dived into the life-giving fluid in the now-opened cooler.

After several bottles, his thirst was slaked, so he got out one more to sip on while he sat and agitated his less-fortunate companions who were still shooting. By the time the field cleared, the two six-packs were "deader'n doornails," the doves were cleaned and packed in ice, and the happy hunter was ready to shower and shave for the Opening Day Party.

There was a line for the shower, so he mixed a highball. Matter of fact, he mixed a couple. And drank them. Plus another one while he dried, shaved, and dressed. Then one more to join the party on. He carried his condition well.

The first inkling we had of how far gone he was, was when we walked into the dining room and found him in front of a plate of barbequed venison, in earnest conversation with a pretty brunette in a very low cut blouse. It was cooked to pieces (the venison, not the hunter nor the contents of the blouse) and our hero was wearing barbeque all down the front of his white shirt. While giving the cleavage all the attention it certainly deserved, he was scooping up his first solid food in twenty-four hours with one hand, but making it to his mouth with maybe half of it. "He looks like he's been field-dressed," observed a companion. And we thought he would be when his wife joined the watching, wondering throng.

107

FIREWATER   I did see a fellow literally struck blind by the overconsumption of firewater once. This was a non-hunter, who came to deer camp for the companionship and to let his hair down. After a night of drinking and cards, he hit the sack about the time everybody else was leaving for the woods. He was still dead to the world when the hunters returned for lunch and someone observed that he had gone to sleep with his glasses on. This someone also noticed a can of spray paint on the window sill. Very carefully, this prankster removed his victim's glasses, spray-painted the lenses black, and replaced them, while the rest of the camp watched. Several hunters then initiated enough obstreperous conduct to awaken the dead—or drunk. Consciousness returned to the man in the bed.

"Oh, my God!" he exclaimed. "I'm blind!" and burst into tears.

It took the better part of an hour, and several hairs of the dog, before the victim could see the humor of the situation. That night, the scene was reenacted time and again, prompting the remark by one former heavy drinker who had gone on the wagon, "Now I remember why I drank so much," he muttered darkly; "It was so I could stand to be around the rest of you so-and-so's!"

There was another time when a man on the wagon was getting a tour of the island with a group of very accomplished drinkers in an open jeep on a cold day. The chill factor necessitated the occasional stopping of the jeep to pass around a bottle of spirits purported to warm both body and soul. The teetotaler's protests were brushed aside by the rough, tough, head of the excursion, who not only had a rifle in the gun rack, but also had a pistol on his belt, both in the event he encountered poachers. "Man who's too good to drink with me is too good to ride with me," he rumbled ominously.

The man on the wagon was a guest, and did not know this individual's callousness was feigned, nor did he know his reputation as a prankster, as did the club members in the jeep. He only knew that he was somewhere on a

108

twelve-thousand-acre island with no idea as to which direction a friendly fire might be. He therefore tilted the bottle to his lips obediently but "tongued" the opening, so that he didn't actually drink any liquor. Uttering a satisfied grunt, he passed the bottle to the next man.

This happened several more times during the tour, and the teetotaler thought he was getting away with the deception until he lifted the bottle to his lips once more. Suddenly, he felt the cold steel of a pistol barrel against his temple and heard the chilling click of the hammer cocking. "I'd better see that Adam's apple workin' this time," the driver declared in a dead-serious voice.

It worked. The man was forever after known as "George Sipper."

There was another George on camp who entered not so unwillingly into a bout with John Barleycorn one night. He *was* unwillingly pulled from his bunk the next morning, though. At the drawing for stands during supper, he had been assigned one of the best stands on the hunt, overlooking a stretch of sandbar that bucks often crossed after being jumped by the dogs and riders on the main island. George's companions hustled the protesting hunter into his clothes and aboard a waiting jeep, which deposited him on the sandy bluff. The dogs and riders were "cast" and the hunt was on!

An hour later, one of the riders came upon George, who was seated against a cottonwood and seemed to cringe at every step the horse made approaching him across the sand. "Hey, didn't that big ten-point cross out here?" the rider hailed.

George winced at the voice and nodded his head carefully, so that it didn't fall off.

The rider now spied the deer's tracks in the sand and pointed. "Damn, he wasn't thirty yards. Why didn't you shoot him?" he exclaimed.

George unleashed a withering glance at the rider and softly patted the 30-06 across his lap.

"Fella, do you have *any idea* how much *noise* this thing makes?!!!"

One of the ways to get the hoss riders to come by your deer stand, thereby insuring some activity in your area, is to let them know that there will be a bottle of firewater in your vehicle parked nearby. Hoss riders are more exposed to the chill factor, so therefore need more warming fluids introduced into their systems at regular intervals. My Uncle Sam, a gregarious soul who enjoyed an evening toddy or two, was hunting with me one morning at the North Rim canebrake, but a new fifth of bourbon on the seat of the Scout failed to troll up any hoss riders. We were on the way to the cabin for lunch when a nice eight-point bounded across the road in front of us and stopped twenty yards on the other side. I slammed on the brakes (miracle of miracles, for once we had brakes!) and cut the wheels left, to give Uncle Sam the shot. Instead, both the buck and I were spooked by his bellow: "Dammit, boy! That was a brand-new bottle of whiskey!"

I think it's called inertia. The bottle, unimpressed by my magnificent braking job, had continued its journey, smashing full-speed into the dashboard. Uncle Sam berated me all the way to camp, and the Scout reeked for weeks.

Uncle Sam was also along on the deep-sea fishing trip when I forgot my Dopp kit. I didn't discover this until the next morning, when we were anchored out at the Chandeleur Islands, and I awoke below decks with no toothbrush, toothpaste, or mouthwash. I went to the galley to find a suitable substitute. Uncle Sam, Uncle Shag, and the mate, Buddy Manuel, were sitting at the table with coffee cups. In the middle of the table was a bottle of bourbon and a bottle of pepper sauce. I decided on the former.

The three men regarded me (a teenager) with suspicious curiosity when I picked up the bottle, uncapped it, took a big swig, recapped it, and set it back on the table. Cheeks puffed out, I swished the stuff around my mouth a few

110

times, stepped out the door, and spit explosively over the rail. Buddy's outraged voice boomed out, "Hey, boy! That's *good* whiskey!"

The next morning when I woke up and came to the galley, he didn't say a word. Just reached over and grabbed the whiskey bottle to clutch it to his bosom.

I don't remember what brand of whiskey that was that Buddy was so protective of, but I have learned that there is no accounting for some people's tastes. There was a time when a neighbor of ours was hosting a dove shoot, which is usually an enjoyable job. He was riding around the pasture in his pickup all afternoon, visiting with friends, transporting hunters in and out of the field, and refreshing them with water, cold drinks, or beer from the coolers in the back of his truck. He was feeling charitable late in the afternoon when he saw an uninvited guest enter the field from a nearby blacktop road. Jamie not only decided to let the trespasser hunt, but he drove over to offer him a ride across the pasture. "Thanks," the fellow said, climbing into the back of the pickup, "I b'lieve I'll try over by them trees."

Jamie agreeably transported the man to the shade, and when the fellow got out of the truck, he thanked the host, "Much obliged. Say, you got any beer in them iceboxes?"

"Sure," Jamie said, "help yourself out of that blue cooler." He sat with the motor running, watching in the rearview mirror as the guy leaned over and began rummaging in the cooler. After about a minute of hearing ice cubes shoved back and forth, he asked, "What's wrong? I'm outa beer?"

"Naw," the disgusted poacher returned, "You ain't got nothin' but Bud in here!"

Jamie's charity disappeared. "Put your butt back in this truck!" the landowner roared. "You don't like my beer, you can hunt somewhere else!"

111

FIREWATER   While I am not opposed to anyone's having a good time, I do feel there is a time and place for liquor, especially a stopping place. Those who get too caught up in having a good time at night often pay the price the next day. Their attitude then can probably best be summed up using an incident that Big Robert reported happening on a deer stand one morning.

A doe spooked by him from the south, long after the dogs and hoss riders had passed his tree stand from that direction. He therefore expected to see a rutting buck behind her, and was rather surprised to see the white horse and its rider plodding slowly toward him. Big Robert watched in silence as the rider reined in his mount next to a big white sycamore log about thirty yards behind the tree stand. The rider dismounted carefully, almost painfully, and climbed onto the log, uttering a long rumbling belch as he seated himself and cradled his face in his hands. Big Robert could smell last night's whiskey even at thirty yards and fifteen feet up a tree. The rider moaned, unaware of any human observers. His sympathetic horse nuzzled the hungover cheek comfortingly. The rider leaned his head on the horse's nose and uttered the words that he is now famous for.

"Horse, I bet you don't feel *near 'bout* as bad as I do!"

Old Guns and Old Dogs

It was an old gun, as guns go, and about shot out, to boot. The blueing was plumb gone from the steel, and the stock was cracked down the grain of the grip. The bottom one-third of the butt plate had been broken slap off just below the screw hole. Probably the same blow had split off the bottom corner of the stock, but the piece that was gone wasn't much longer than a man's thumbnail and it didn't affect the balance of the gun.

The boy was eight years old and had about grown big enough for the old sixteen-gauge Model Twelve that had been his grandaddy's. He had been shooting a little twenty gauge single-shot that I had cut the stock down on, but had about outgrown it. Looked like it was about time to cast about for another gun.

The old Winchester had been the only gun his grandfather had ever hunted with. It had been purchased with World War I discharge pay and had shot at many a quail, dove, duck, rabbit, and squirrel over the next six decades. It had never been a hang-on-the-wall gun; it was a wipe-down-with-an-oily-rag-and-stand-in-the-kitchen-corner gun. It belonged to be shot out at its age.

The head space was so enlarged that I could not shoot the little sixteen. I shoot left-handed, so caught the escaping blast effect right in the face. The grandfather had been right-handed, though, and so was the boy, and they could get by without being bothered by the worn-out chamber. It scared me to let a kid shoot it, however, and I was just before hanging it on the wall.

But that fall, just on a whim, I decided it wouldn't hurt to at least ask. Retiring a good gun or a good dog is not a decision to be made lightly. There is

115

a difference, though: the dog will keep on going until it cannot go anymore, and then soon it will die and be buried with tears and fond memories. Any hunter who cares to think about it will know that his dog's passing is merely a look into a future mirror. One day the hunter, too, will grow old and be unable to go back to the woods, and then soon he will die, and the tears and fond memories will be for him. It's the way of the world; we can't change it.

An old and treasured gun, however, is a machine made of wood and steel, and many times when it gets worn out, we can take it to a skilled craftsman and have it restored to working order. Maybe the reason we do that is in subconscious rebellion against the system that has taken our dogs and old friends away from us, and that we know will one day get us too. Certainly we all know that new technology permits the construction of better weapons today than sixty years ago. But when we get out of bed on fall mornings sounding like a bowl of Rice Krispies (Snap! Crackle! Pop!) because of football shoulders, basketball knees, baseball ankles, and tennis elbows—that is when we decide to have old guns rebuilt. It's our only way to fight the system.

The insurance on the package was considerably more than adequate. The accompanying letter was a model of simplicity. It said:

Dear Mr. Winchester,

This old gun has shot a heap of shells through it and seems to be on its last legs. But if there's any way it can be made safe and suitable to go under the Christmas tree for an eight-year-old, I'd like to know it.

I don't remember the guy's name who wrote back, (no, I don't work for Winchester; you would probably get the same service out of Mr. Remington, Mr. Browning, or any other gun company) but he wrote a mighty nice letter saying all it needed was a barrel sleeve (or chamber sleeve?) for about four bucks. Said if it was his, he'd get a new firing pin for another four or five bucks; and since it was for an eight-year-old's Christmas, he'd love for me to let him

116

put a blue job on it. I said okay, sent the nice fellow his money, and had the little gun back by Thanksgiving. It took me another two weeks to refinish the stock and forearm myself, but when I got through, there wasn't a prettier piece of work in the world.

The hardest part was waiting until Christmas to give it to the boy.

Probably a dozen times after watching him shooting the single-shot, I made up my mind to go ahead and give it to him early. Each time I successfully resisted the temptation, or else my wife talked me out of it. I was a relieved soul when Christmas Eve came and the long wrapped box could come out of the closet and go under the tree.

When I was a kid, my mother used to make us slit the tape and unwrap the packages carefully, so she could fold the paper to reuse for birthdays, anniversaries, or the next Christmas. That practice doesn't work on our kids. Spoiled 'em, I guess. The boy lit into that paper like a duck on a June bug, but the enthusiasm changed to awe when he opened the box.

He knew this gun. It had belonged to his mother's father, whom he was named for, and she had tears in her eyes as she watched him pause reverently and then reach out to touch the old Model Twelve. He ran his fingers lightly down the newly blued barrel, then wiped it with his sleeve. The varnish gleamed like it was wet, so he reached out gingerly to touch the forearm, afraid he would leave a print. Satisfied that it was dry, he finally, ever so carefully, picked it up and checked the breech. (What a present for me on Christmas! He had learned something right!) He could just barely shoulder it, and sighted at a red ball hanging from the tree. He intended no disrespect to the Three Wise Men depicted on the brightly-colored ball.

Matter of fact, maybe he understood a little better.

And a Merry Christmas to you, Mr. Winchester!

Early Arrivals

Back Water Green Heads

Wood Ducks

Flooded Timber Flight

First Pair

"**W**ell, they're baggy at the knees, they're baggy in the seat, and there are three folds between the crotch and the knee!" I thought my wife was being overly critical. Then she grinned, "But I'll bet you can't get him out of them!"

The subject of her fashion critique was a ten-year-old boy parading around the Christmas tree in his jockey shorts and brand new waders. We live in a rural part of the state, so it had not been easy to find a child's pair of waders, but I had done the best I could. Suspenders had not been a problem at all. We had just taken the laces out of his sneakers and tied them straight across each shoulder.

"If they'll keep the water out, that's all that matters," I told the lady of the house. "I may have to put bricks in those folds to keep him from floating!"

Christmas afternoon down at the swimming hole the boy checked his new waders for leaks and for floating. They did neither. There was a brief argument about how long he needed for testing purposes. I won.

First there was a deer hunt the two of us had to get out of the way, so it was after the first of the year before we could test the new waders on ducks. The weather had still not turned very cold, so there were not a lot of big ducks down yet. But there were woodies aplenty in the swamp a mile or so from the house. The boy and I waded in to an opening where I knew they liked to roost.

The water was waist deep on the boy. I tried to show him the wading-in-flooded-woods technique of cautiously sliding his feet, being careful to keep the weight on the back foot until the front foot was firmly planted. His .16

121

gauge Model 12 was held crossways for balance, and I instructed him carefully on how he was to hold the barrel and shove the butt into the mud to catch himself should he trip. I learned this method by example when I was not much older than the boy.

I had accompanied my father and three other men on a hunting trip where we had to wade several hundred yards of flooded woods to reach the blind. One of the men was very short, and his waders fit him about like the boy's did. There was a lot of room in them for air to be trapped. In addition, Buddy wore a shell belt strapped tightly across his chest. He was about fifteen yards from the nearest hunter when he stepped in the stump hole and disappeared.

Well, all of him didn't disappear for very long. His feet almost immediately popped to the surface. A second later a gun barrel appeared with two gloved hands climbing it. Buddy's head broke water, gasping. "Help!" he yelled, and grabbed a breath. The head vanished again as the air-filled boots popped back up. Once more the gloves climbed the barrel. The face was a little pop-eyed this time, I thought. "Whuff!" he gasped, and went back under. The hands began a third assent, and when the head surfaced again, another hunter had gotten there to rescue him.

The boy laughed when I told the story, but I could tell by the way he looked at his gun that he was going to have to get wet the first time, anyway. The little Model 12 had been his grandfather's and dated from the 1920s. The kid wasn't fixing to stick it in the mud.

We waded about two hundred yards from the gravel road to a huge moss-covered cypress log I knew about. Acorns, pecans, and pignuts floated all around us. And feathers—there were lots of feathers on the surface. The wood ducks had been using this place. The boy and I settled down on the log. "Now when they come in, there're gonna be a wad of 'em all at once," I instructed. "Pick one duck; don't shoot the whole bunch. If he's coming down, shoot at his feet. If he's going up, shoot at his bill." The boy nodded.

122

To the east, behind us, we could hear an occasional squeal of a woody. I explained the noise and the reason these ducks are called "squealers" locally. A stray mallard would high-ball back in the swamp once in a while. In whispers I pointed out the difference in the sounds of various kinds of ducks. The boy listened, big-eyed.

The sun began to drop below the trees. A screech owl began its haunting, high-pitched, shivering call. Another answered somewhere behind us. I identified the sound in a low whisper. A squirrel began cutting a nut in the tree over them, and little pieces sprinkled on the boy's end of the log. He grinned and pointed them out. Questioningly, he also indicated a pile of dung on the end of the log. " 'Coon. Been eating hackberries," I mouthed.

"Maybe we'll see him," the boy said hopefully under his breath.

Back to the north, toward the canal, a bobcat squalled. That set off a great horned owl. "Who—who—whowho; who—who—whoWHOOO!" it hooted. The screech owls talked to each other, and a third entered the conversation from a sweetgum right in front of us. I tried to show the boy the little bird silhouetted on a limb, but he could never make it out.

The sun had dropped below the trees when we heard the first squealers approaching from the east. I nudged the boy, who scanned the treetops moving only his eyes and frowned. He could see nothing.

Then, in a rush of wings, the ducks were upon us. There must have been fifty in the flock. Wood ducks dropped through the trees all around the cypress log and splashed into the water. The boy froze. Seems like every duck squealed as it settled. A drake not six feet behind us shrieked, and both of us had to control our tendency to jump. The drake swam by the boy's end of the log, stuck its head in the drift, and shoveled in a pignut. The kid stifled a grin.

We sat like the proverbial bumps on a log.

Woodies fed all around us, quieter now, their squeals no longer a cacophony. The squirrel came down the tree, hopped onto the log, and was within arm's

123

reach of the boy when it apparently smelled us. It sat up on its hind legs to study us, then retreated back down the log and jumped onto the tree trunk. The bushy-tail perched on a lower limb and chirred at these intruders to its territory. A big barred owl, obviously attracted by the squirrel's noise, slipped in on silent wings and lit in the tree. The squirrel shut up and flattened out on the branch. After a few moments, the owl uttered its low-pitched casual "Whoooo." The monkey-like face regarded us humans suspiciously, then just as silently as it had come, the owl departed. The squirrel almost audibly breathed a sigh of relief.

Another smaller bunch of woodies dropped in. The boy never knew he had a gun across his lap. Our trio of screech owls resumed their conversation, joined by an occasional squealer. A fox yapped out at the field edge of the woods. Somewhere deep in the swamp behind us a hound bayed faintly. The ducks quieted down and began feeding off to the east.

We sat on the cypress until slap-black dark. Neither of us wanted to break the spell. Finally I nudged the boy and whispered, "Ready?" He nodded.

A couple of close ducks flushed and flew maybe fifty yards when we stood. The sweetgum screech owl put the tree trunk between himself and us. We heard the squirrel's claws on the bark as he went around and up the pecan. I had not brought a flashlight, so it was a slow wade back to the road. We got too close to a beaver and nearly jumped out of our boots when it slapped the water with its tail.

I didn't have to ask the boy why he had not shot; I knew, and somehow was vaguely proud of him. Back at the truck, I helped him out of his waders and remarked casually, "They'll be back for a little while early in the morning. You want to come down for an hour or so before we have to get ready for Sunday School?" The boy nodded. "Yessir!"

It was clear as a bell when I pitched the coffee grounds out the back door the

next morning. The boy and I had a quick bowl of cereal before leaving and I carried my third cup of coffee to the pickup. The boy made sure we had a flashlight. We jumped a couple of deer on the ditchbank when we entered the swamp. One of the deer blew at us a dozen times. "Goin' back to the log?" the boy asked.

"Yep."

"Good. I like that place."

We were able to cut the flashlight off before we reached the log. Day was breaking fast. When we settled down on our moss-covered seat, the boy excitedly showed me evidence that the 'coon had been back during the night. Two of the screech owls spoke to us. Squeals of woodies sounded in the distance.

"Remember, now. When they come in, pick one duck. When he's coming down, shoot at his feet."

Duck hunting is a lot like turkey hunting. Just when you think you've got them figured out, they change their game plan. The first flock of ducks came from behind. The lead drake passed us, dropped his left wing, banked, and dove through the trees headfirst. The boy's gun was up, and he threw me a quick perplexed look over his gunstock.

The drake swooped down below the sweetgum branches, made a swing back up, locked all the brakes, and started his splash down.

The boy busted him.

The rest of the flock had been just off the water. A second drake directly over the first one flared frantically. The boy pumped and swung. The .16 barked again and the drake folded. A double on his first ducks!

"Good shootin'!" I exclaimed, thumping him on the back, just as excited as he was. "Go pick 'em up!"

The boy handed me the little Winchester and pushed himself off the cypress.

125

His sloshing progress toward the ducks put up a bow wave.

"Slow down," I laughed. "they're not goin' anywhere! You're gonna trip and dunk yourself." The kid slowed down fractionally.

Most hunters would have picked the woodies up by the neck, but not the boy. Gently, almost reverently, he slipped a hand under each drake and lifted them from the water. His glance went from one to the other as he waded slowly back, grinning from ear to ear. He let me hold one while he boosted himself back onto the mossy log.

There's probably not anything quite as colorful and beautiful as a wood duck drake. A big old irridescent, red-headed gobbler is close, but that fire-engine red head loses its color when you shoot him. The little painted buntings that migrate in with their indigo cousins are not as colorful as a woody. A just-come-south mallard drake with green head, yellow bill, russet chest, blue chevron, and orange feet is almost as impressive, you'll have to admit. Many hunters prefer the sedate good looks of an old bull pintail, who's like a gentleman in a tuxedo. Some folks say a wood duck drake is gaudy, but maybe God just made them pretty and put them here for a little boy's first duck.

The boy, now seated on the log with me, held out his hand. Somehow, I knew he didn't want the .16 back. I carefully laid the drake in the outstretched palm, and propped its head up as best I could. The young hunter held each duck up in turn and slowly rotated his wrist, studying each feather, each bit of color carefully.

There's a colloquialism down here that covers it well: the boy "mirated" over those two wood duck drakes.

Do you ever think older hunters maybe get a little hardened to the wonders of nature? That we sometimes take for granted the everyday things that are thrilling to an amateur? When's the last time you just stopped and studied the

126

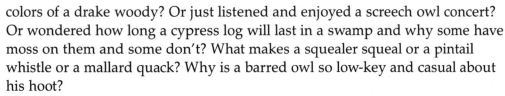

colors of a drake woody? Or just listened and enjoyed a screech owl concert? Or wondered how long a cypress log will last in a swamp and why some have moss on them and some don't? What makes a squealer squeal or a pintail whistle or a mallard quack? Why is a barred owl so low-key and casual about his hoot?

Then, on the other hand, maybe that's one of the reasons we go to the woods: because we can just accept these things and don't *have* to think about them. That's not a good enough explanation for a ten-year-old, though.

The sun peeped over the trees and bathed in its gleaming light a kid in camouflage sitting on a mossy green log holding two wood duck drakes. The moss shined, the ducks shined, the boy's eyes shined. Why do hunters never have the camera when we need it?

One by one, the boy set the ducks in the water and carefully propped their heads back. He pushed them gently from him. One of the heads drooped into the water and he used a stick to retrieve the drake and gently set the head back up. With the stick he "swam" the ducks slowly in front of him.

Another flock lit in, but he never reached for the gun. Woodies swam around the log, but kept their distance in the daylight. A hen thirty yards away fed into a drift and gulped down seven pecans in a row. The boy half-stifled an amazed chuckle that flushed the hen and a dozen others. I could see I was going to have to explain gizzards on the way back.

I basked in the sun's warmth like an old turtle and watched the boy play with his two drakes. The moss was cool and almost furry to my touch. The local squirrel began to gnaw a nut, sprinkling us with the cuttings. A movement up in the sweetgum revealed a possum. I showed it to the boy.

We faintly heard the whistle at the oil works six miles away in town. I punched the youngster. "C'mon, let's go show those woodies to your mother."

127

He grinned and nodded and picked up his ducks. I could see that the boy wasn't going to have enough hands. "I'll carry your gun," I volunteered, and unloaded both pumps.

Back at the house, after all the "mirations" and congratulations were over, I was tying my tie when I heard my wife call to one of the kids, "Hurry up or we'll be late for church!"

I grinned at myself in the mirror. I felt like maybe a couple of us had already been.

The McElwee Hoist

Once upon a time Big Robert and I were casting for bass on one of the small "river-run" lakes on The Island. I was sculling the little twelve-foot john boat, with Big Robert in the back and our guest between us. This guest was one of those bass fishermen with a capital "A," and he was fishing a plastic worm. Big Robert usually didn't put up with this kind of foolishness, but he was busy rigging his own rod; since we had barely left the landing, neither of us had noticed the technique our comrade was using.

Suddenly, this bass fisherman (with a capital "A") dropped his rod tip to the water, reeled up the slack, and carefully lifted the rod, feeling the fish. Then without warning, in one motion he more or less jumped to his feet and gave a mighty lunge to set the hook!

Twelve-foot john boats were never designed for mighty lunges.

Big Robert and I reacted instinctively, leaning forward to try to counter-balance the mighty lunge from this bass fisherman with a capital "A". At the same time, Big Robert roared in a bellow that blew down three willows between us and the bank, "Dammit, Boy! SIT DOWN IN MY BOAT!!!"

The bass fisherman with a capital "A" obeyed so quickly that we shipped water before Big Robert and I could quit counterbalancing, and the two-pound bass, given slack, spit out the worm. My elder picked his pocket knife up off the seat and wordlessly reached out a long arm to cut the line of the rod of the bass fisherman with a capital "A". Still without a word, he picked up a spinner bait and handed it to the man, who meekly tied it on. It was two hours before

131

Big Robert regained his normal good humor. The bass fisherman with a capital "A" missed strikes the rest of the afternoon because he seemed afraid to set the hook. I thought the whole thing was funny.

At the time I was a novice at bass fishing and was unfamiliar with the type of fisherman who can only function with one of those floating fiberglass platforms that has at least a hundred horses on the back. Not only is "scull" an unknown tongue to these fishermen, but I have had to explain "paddle" to a couple of them. Theirs is an entirely new vocabulary; for instance, they have no concept of "cork" unless used in the connotation of stopping up a wine bottle. "Stringer" has been replaced by "live well"; "pull cord" by "starter button"; and as far as I know, "beer" has been superceded by "champagne". I have yet to learn all the language.

I was brought up in a fly fishing family, and have spent many an hour on many a lake after bream with Big Robert, Uncle Sam, Cousin Fitz, and Sammy Shaifer. If the bass started hitting around us, we just tied on a bigger bug with a heavier leader. Once, on some kind of promotion at the hardware store, I won a spinning rod with an open-face reel. After that, I acquired a few bass lures and considered myself a bass fisherman.

Until one afternoon Dude and I hit the Alligator Hole after a six-inch rain. In three hours, we filled our stringer with bass, keeping none under three pounds. Problem was, he beat me at least two to one. Not at hooking fish, but at putting them in the boat. Dude was using a stiff rod with an Ambassadeur reel and really put me to shame. I'd cast with my light tackle between two stumps, a six-pounder would smash the spinner bait, I'd stick him, and the fish would go around a stump to throw the lure. Dude would cast at the same fish between the stumps, jerk the bass cross-eyed when he set the hook, and boat it in the same motion. That evening, he made me a present of his rod and reel,

132

and in return I gratefully named this new-found technique "The McElwee Hoist."

Basically, the McElwee Hoist boasts only two rules: 1) "When in doubt, stick it!"; and 2) "If you want to play a fish, play it on the stringer."

To master the Hoist, jerk the rod tip straight up (without gaining your feet!) and reel as hard and fast as possible until the fish is in the boat. Using the McElwee Hoist, I have successfully boated bass who had only intended to nibble at the skirt of a spinner bait; I had them in the boat before they could reopen their mouth. Dude once boated one that had just come by for a smell!

Sometimes this technique can be dangerous, though. If you have just run over a stick or some other obstruction that activates Rule 1 of the McElwee Hoist, bear in mind that a fast dodge may be necessary. Once a fishing partner did the Hoist while fishing a large size jointed lure with three gangs of treble hooks. He missed the fish, but didn't duck quickly enough; the lure hit him smack between the eyes, broadside, and stuck!

"I'm blind!" he screamed to his boat partner, and sure enough, he was. At least, temporarily. The middle gang was hooked on the bridge of his nose, and the other two gangs had fastened his reflex-closed eyelids securely to his cheeks. The resulting blood trickling from beneath the eyelids helped his partner reach an immediate decision: "We're goin' to find a doctor! You just set still!"

It took a half-hour for them to get to the landing, carefully disembark (the boat partner did cut the victim's line), load everything into the truck (one man doing the loading, of course), and drive to the doctor's home in the little river town. The doctor was an elderly man who obviously knew his business, for he quickly and carefully ascertained without removing the lure that the fisherman's eyes had not been damaged; the hooks had merely gone through the lids

133

and into the skin of the cheeks. Both fishermen were visibly relieved.

The old doctor sat the victim down and tenderly swabbed off the dried blood; then he pulled himself up a chair and seated himself knee to knee with his patient. "Son," he said, "I'll get this out directly. But if you don't mind, I just want to *look* at you for a spell. In all my years, I b'lieve this is the most int'restin' accident I've ever treated!"

I did almost the same thing one time while I was fishing with Jody, except I had one leg propped up on the boat transom, and both gangs of treble hooks on the Big O latched on just above my knee. I bit my lip, laid my rod down, picked up my pocketknife, and began self-surgery. In the front of the boat, Jody was busy sculling and casting, so he didn't notice my predicament, since I had not yelled or cussed.

I have had lots of practice over the years at bleeding; it is something I do really well. I had gotten four of six hooks loose and was making real progress on the fifth, when my partner turned and saw my blood-covered bare leg. He turned white as a sheet and nearly dropped his rod.

"My God, man! Why didn't you say something!" he gasped, and then dived for the ice chest in the middle of the boat. He jerked a clean handkerchief out of his pocket and soaked it in the icy water, at the same time removing a cold can of "RC" from the cooler. "Now *there's* a real buddy!" I thought appreciatively. "It's nice to fish with somebody that looks out after you."

Jody popped the top off the cold drink and drained half of it in one long swallow. He flopped back onto the front seat and dropped the cold wet hanky across his brow before taking another gulp. "You got to be more careful, fella," he admonished. "I get faint at the sight of blood!"

This same companion was the instigator of one of the most spectacular Hoists I have ever seen. A combination of beavers and wind had felled a sycamore tree into the lake, but enough roots were still attached that it stayed green and leafy.

Jody cast into the edge of this tree, and his Christmas Tree Dive Bomber went a little too far, wrapping one time around a thumb-thick limb. The lure dangled just above the water for a few seconds, then just as he tried to flip it loose, a real bucketmouth erupted from the lake and inhaled the Bomber!

Jody laid the McElwee Hoist on him!

The bass, which later proved to weigh eight pounds, was jerked slap out of the water. Jody's rod bent nearly double. The sycamore limb positioned between rod and fish hardly bent at all.

Alerted by Jody's incoherent stuttering, I took in the situation at a glance and reeled in quickly. The bass was flopping as madly as possible while snubbed open-mouthed up to a sycamore limb three feet out of the water. Jody was still involved in Hoisting. It was obvious that if I didn't do something quick, either rod or line would break. I grabbed the paddle and hollered, "Get the net! I'll run your end into the tree. Keep a tight line!" (When we got home, I went and bought some of that brand line.)

Jody kept a tight line and the big fish stayed hooked until I got the boat positioned. Rod held high, my companion stuck the net under the bass without even getting the rim wet. He then lowered the rod and brought the net into the boat; but the line was still wrapped around the limb. The excited fisherman had netted the biggest bass of his career, but he still had major problems.

I watched with amusement as the net would come in and the rod would go out; then the rod would come in and the net would go out; back and forth continued the contest. The bass was still hooked and flopping, the rod was bent double, and Jody was getting more and more exasperated and panicky. I pulled out my knife to help. "Lemme cut the line," I suggested, leaning forward.

I've never been exactly sure what my friend thought I meant by that, but it

135

pushed him over the edge. "Nooooo!" he screamed—and began getting out of the boat and into the tree!

Well, I did calm him down and keep both fish and fisherman in the boat. He compromised by letting me cut the limb. I kept it in the boat so he could mount it with the fish.

Big Robert rarely got shook up in this manner, but one day on the Alligator Hole, Dude and I witnessed my sire pushed to his limit. He was fishing a black Shannon Spinner and had cast it up to the edge of the bank. As he eased the lure into the shallow water, a wake similar to a shark's boiled out from behind a nearby stump and charged the lure. The fish came out of the water as it smashed its prey, and it weighed at least ten pounds. It was the biggest bass any of us had ever seen; and the fastest. It grabbed the Shannon and bolted for open water, headed right for the boat.

Big Robert executed the Hoist, but the line was coming toward him too fast and he couldn't get enough slack out to set the hook. Long arms straight up, he reeled frantically, but to no avail. The huge fish raced under the boat and out into the lake, and the line tightened only briefly before it snapped against the side of the boat. We all three sat breathless for a frozen moment, then exhaled and cussed simultaneously. Dude and I commiserated with our elder, who was shaking visibly as he tried to light a cigarette. What a fish!

Finally, the two of us at each end of the boat went back to casting as Big Robert, still muttering under his breath, rummaged in his tackle box for another Shannon Spinner and a snap swivel. He found one of each, opened the safety pin-like snap with difficulty, slipped the pin through the eye of the Shannon, and clipped it secure. Then he dropped the secured lure into the water and picked up his rod.

And realized he had never tied the swivel to his line.

136

This realization froze him for a few seconds, then without saying a word or moving, he carefully cut his eyes left and right to see if his boat partners had taken note of his befuddled error.

We had, but we knew better than to admit it until we knew whether our elder was really going to explode or not. He obviously was inclined to do so initially, but the humor of the situation finally got to him, and for the rest of the afternoon (indeed, for years afterward when the three of us fished together) we would always giggle when dropping a Shannon Spinner into the water before casting.

A final word on The McElwee Hoist: do not use it while fly fishing. For several summers after Dude had broken me in, I turned to bass fishing almost exclusively. Therefore, when an older man invited me to accompany him fly fishing for bream, I accepted, but was a little rusty on my fly rodding techniques. We had only been on the lake about an hour when a three or four pound bass darted out from behind a cypress and smashed my popping bug. Instinctively, I put the McElwee Hoist on him.

The eight foot fly rod broke plumb in two, three feet up from my hands.

Well, we tried to splint and bandage the unfortunate victim, but it was a long afternoon; especially with the chuckles and giggles coming off and on from the other end of the boat. It took me exactly one week to silence my companion. I'm not sure I could have stood it much longer.

We were again fly fishing, but had our bass rods in the boat. Suddenly, every bass in the lake seemed to go on a feeding frenzy. I already had a red-and-white Shannon Spinner on my rod, so I picked it up and flipped at the nearest ripples. The lure had hardly hit the water when a six-pounder socked it.

Mr. Albert could hardly wait to net my fish before he began to rig his rod. I had two more bass in the boat before he made his first cast. He put a lot of body English into his motion, so was leaning out over the water with his rod at arm's length when the lure hit the water.

The reel handle fell off, and hardly made a ripple where it sank.

It was a long afternoon for him, too.

No, I did not. I swear it.

Paddles: The Long and Short of It

It was one of those still foggy mornings on the Mississippi River. Beau and I had gotten on the small lake at first light and were maybe two hundred yards down from the landing, casting spinner baits for bass. Foggy mornings like these seem extra silent: not only do you hate to speak, but you're careful not to let paddle, rod, or lure bump the boat lest the noise break the spell. There had been no sound since we left the landing save the muted ripple of his sculling and the barely audible whirr of our reels. Only occasionally did I have to use my paddle to swing my end of the boat back straight. I had just picked it up to do that very thing as we crossed an old flooded road.

The road was a straight, clear lane through the willows to the bank fifty feet away. But you don't look at the bank while you're fishing unless some sound or movement attracts your attention. The ten-foot alligator lying on the bank had not attracted our attention whatsoever, nor apparently had we attracted his, until the big reptile obviously thought that the boat across this clear lane to the open lake was an attempt to trap him in the shallow water. He made a break for freedom—right toward us.

I know that the movement gained our notice before the splash, because both of us were under the impression that we were being attacked by the twenty-foot alligator charging down the bank. The splash closely resembled that made by a nuclear submarine I had seen launched several years previously. Beau and I needed no further incentive to drop our bass rods and paddle madly to get out of the thirty-foot monster's path. If we moved at all, it was in very, very slow motion. The behemoth's bow wave surged toward us, and I remembered scenes from some old African movie (maybe *King Solomon's Mines?*) that showed a hippo surging up out of the river with a whole canoe, at least two native men, the cook tent, and two months' safari supplies gripped gruesomely in his gleaming ivories. The hippo seemed somewhat small compared to this forty-foot Mississippi leviathan. So did the nuclear submarine, for that matter.

Despite our best efforts, we couldn't get the tiny twelve-foot boat out of the way of the fire-breathing fifty-foot scaly beast. We tensed at the last second and squinched our eyes shut, breathlessly awaiting the grinding crunch of the fearsome jaws that would snuff out our young lives. The 'gator closed for the kill.

And went under the boat.

Not feeling crunched or swallowed, I peeked fearfully out from under my cap bill. Beau was doing the same. The alligator had missed us and continued his escape into deeper waters. We both exhaled with a sigh, then took deep breaths. My brother turned slowly to me and spoke carefully and deliberately:

"Next time we need to get away from anything—let's both paddle in the *same direction!*"

I noticed that for the rest of that summer he unobtrusively went one step further: he only took one paddle to the boat. Sometimes this can work to your disadvantage, though.

Like the time Big Robert and Dan ran over to the lake for a few hours fishing one afternoon. They ended up somehow with only one short sculling paddle and Dan, being the youngest, got to scull the boat. They were doing fine until they invaded the territory of a five foot cottonmouth moccasin.

Many times Mississippi River moccasins labor under the belief that they actually own territorial rights on certain ponds and lakes, and a fisherman must be careful in deciding to dispute these rights. Dan was not careful enough. As the big moccasin advanced toward the boat, swimming with his head and two feet of body out of the water, Dan feinted at him with the paddle.

142

The snake hissed belligerently, and declined to back down one iota. Dan drew back with the paddle again as Big Robert noted the impending fracus. "You better let that snake alone," the older man cautioned mildly.

"I ain't scareda no snake," his companion replied. Having said that, he leaned forward and aimed a mighty swat at his antagonist. The snake dodged.

As a rule, fisherman who use short paddles have wet hands. Store-bought paddles also are usually sanded and varnished to a slick finish. The combination of these two factors was Dan's undoing; though his forceful swing missed the snake, his follow-through was everything a coach could wish for. The slick paddle slipped out of his wet hand and sailed majestically ten feet up on the bank, which was fifty feet away.

"Dammit, boy!" roared Big Robert. "I *told* you to leave that snake alone!"

The moccasin commenced to circling the boat ("kinda like th' Injuns circlin' th' wagon train," Dan said later) as the two fishermen drew back their rods— the only weapons they had left. After a couple of circuits of the boat, the snake broke off the engagement and swam back to the bank, head held high in victory.

There, he crawled up on the bank and coiled up—on the paddle!

"What're we gonna do now?" wailed Dan.

"Well, son," the elder man spoke grimly, "you're the one chunked our paddle up on the bank. Now, looks like you're gonna hafta decide whether you're scareder of me or that snake!"

Needless to say, Dan leaned over the bow of the boat and hand paddled to the bank, then broke off a willow limb and went after the big moccasin.

Whenever I've been fishing with my godfather, I've made it a habit to keep several paddles around. On days when the snakes are out in force, I've seen Frank spend more time killing snakes than fishing. He's very empathic about his feud with the serpents, to the extent that he breaks a couple of paddles

143

every trip, seems like. Dude's the same way at times. But every now and then he'll make an exception.

Like the day we were fishing the Alligator Hole for bass. On the bank next to one promising looking little inlet was a huge cottonmouth. I mean, a real champ. I was sculling the boat, so I spotted the moccasin before I cast and purposely passed up the inlet. Dude was not as generous, though, and cast closer and closer to the snake, which just coiled up on the bank and glowered at us.

"That's a belligerent son-of-a-gun," my companion observed, belligerently himself.

"Yeh," I muttered agreement, and kept sculling. I've always had a treaty with snakes; if they'll leave me alone, I'll leave them alone. But I've seen Dude snag them deliberately with a lure, drag them to the boat, and flail the hell out of them with a paddle. These confrontations make me nervous.

My fears were realized. I heard the dreaded declaration, "That sucker needs a lesson!" from the back of the boat. I sighed and reeled in as Dude picked up his sculling paddle and reversed our direction back toward the moccasin. Sensing danger, the cottonmouth hissed and rose warningly from his coils.

"That's one of the biggest snakes I've ever seen, Dude," I observed. "Let's just leave him be."

"Nah," my comrade said scathingly. "You just paddle my end of the boat in there and I'll show him who's boss!"

As I eased the stern toward the snake, Dude raised his paddle and poised to strike. Now I couldn't see past him to tell where his target was. "Guide me; I can't see past you," I said.

"Little closer," he ordered. I gave another stroke.

"Little bit more," he said. I could see him tense as I stroked again. I dragged the blade in the water, ready to back out.

144

"Back up just a hair," my navigator requested. I hit it a lick.

"Little bit more," he said, still tensed. I stroked again.

"One more time," was his order. I backed another stroke. That was what he was waiting for.

Dude swung to face me and applied his paddle to the task for which it had been designed. "Now let's get the hell outa here," he commanded. "That snake's too damn big to hit with this li'l ole paddle!"

I became a permanent fan of short paddles when I was a teenager. Troy and I had invited a town kid to accompany us frog gigging in a little canal on the plantation. This kid was sitting on the middle seat holding a standard five-foot paddle, when a snake dropped out of an overhanging limb into the boat. Me, Troy, and the snake all three learned that there are very few places in a twelve-foot boat that an enthusiastic boy standing on the middle seat cannot reach with a good stout five-foot paddle. I do not buy long paddles any more.

It wasn't funny at the time, but this policy was also espoused by a friend of ours who was a game warden. One summer day, the warden sat back in the shade of some big cypresses and observed with binoculars as three men took more than their limits of white perch from a lake hot spot. When the men decided to leave, the warden cranked up and followed them to the dock where their vehicle was parked. No one else was around the little-used landing, and the lawbreakers pulled into one side of the narrow four-foot-high pier as the warden pointed his boat toward the opposite side. One of the men vaulted onto the pier, holding his rod, tackle box, and a long paddle, just as the warden cut his motor, stood, and reached to grab the dock.

"Well, boys," he greeted them, "I 'spect I'll need to check those fish."

The response was instantaneous from the man above him. Dropping his box and rod, the outlaw grabbed the paddle with both hands, stepped, and swung. The warden was knocked head over heels into the bottom of the boat. He

145

recovered, reached for his pistol, and the man on the dock slammed the paddle into his arm, breaking it. The other two men grabbed all their gear and ran for their truck. The warden tried to raise himself, only to be met with a blow to the head from the relentless weapon.

"Get everything loaded! I'll keep him down!" the paddle wielder yelled to his partners in crime. The warden tried to protect his head from the blows that rained from the dock. Finally, he heard the yell, "C'mon, let's go!" He tried to at least get a look to identify the vehicle, but all he saw were stars from a final blow. The outlaws got clean away.

A week or so later, my father and I went to visit the victim, who was a good friend of ours. During the course of the conversation, Big Robert made the remark, "I bet while you were down in that boat you were wishin' you could get to your gun!"

I'll never forget the warden's answer. Shaking his head grimly, he replied through clenched teeth, "Nope! I was wishin' that son-of-a-bitch had a short paddle!"

Frog-Gigging

I understand that nowadays there is a season on gigging frogs, and that there are bag limits and rules on how the amphibians may or may not be taken. I disremember whether the frogs were infected by such bureaucratic intercedence in my youth, but I know we never paid any attention to it. In the early spring, when it started warming up and you began seeing snakes, the grown-ups set their mouths for froglegs and sent us chullen frog-gigging.

Aesthetically, there's a lot to be said for being afloat in the great outdoors under a bright and starry sky. Your hearing becomes your primary sense: the "riiick, riiick" of the spring peepers, the "chug-a-rum!" of bullfrogs, the sharp slapping splash of an alarmed beaver, the yip of a fox, the hoot of an owl, the cat-like meow of a nutria. You smell the heavy musk of the beaver; the tangy, acidic odor of his freshly gnawed willow sticks; the cold, muddy smell of the sluggish stream.

Realistically, there's a little to be said against being afloat in a narrow brushy creek on a pitch-black night: snakes.

A frog-gigger who has never had a snake in the boat just ain't frog-gigged an awful lot. I normally shy away from dogmatic statements like that, but it happens to me so regularly that it's hard to believe everybody else doesn't have the same problem. On the other hand, if there is such a thing as a law of averages, I'd have to admit that my own experience would necessarily dictate that somewhere there's a dedicated frog hunter who has never *seen* a snake.

Generally, a snake in the boat used to dictate that there be no boys in the same boat. The standard drill was for us to bail out at the first soft "plunk" of a serpent's body unfolding from his low branch into our craft. The water, after all, was hardly ever more than waist deep, and all of us knew that a moccasin could not bite underwater. Our theory was that if he opened his mouth to bite us, he would drown. We were in high school before a concerned science teacher exploded this myth, even obtaining a film from somewhere or other that featured an underwater photographer actually filming a cottonmouth sinking his fangs into a catfish.

I know the teacher meant well, but I was soon to wish that he had left us secure in our ignorance. A few weeks later, Little John, Charles, and I were out gigging a few bullfrogs in a narrow, brushy canal when sure enough, a three-foot stumptail moccasin dropped smack into the middle of the center seat. The fact that this seat was at the same time being occupied by Charles didn't help matters. Charles shrieked and landed on top of me on the rear seat before the echos of that first shriek had died. He started on a second scream and grabbed the little .22 we kept for emergencies, as John and I grasped our first inkling of the extent of his panic. We yelled a useless warning.

This star athelete and scholar, who in college was known for his coolness and ability to hit a curve ball with men on base, or to turn a double play in clutch situations; who would later become a paragon of justice, calm and collected in the heat of a courtroom battle; this older-than-us and looked-up-to companion . . . stood on the boat seat emitting his hoarse battle cry and emptied a ten-shot clip into the snake in the bottom of the boat.

He did kill the snake.

Almost as hard on equipment is the member of the party who picks up a paddle and frenziedly goes to work on similar unwelcome visitors. A guest—a one-time guest—that Troy and I invited to accompany us one night had a snake (a garter snake, at that) bounce off his back during a swift descent from the tree limb. The boy grabbed a paddle and jumped to a stance on the middle seat, from whence he commenced to flail the offending reptile, which really just wanted out of the boat. So did me and Troy. Before the frantic maniac tired, he had demolished flashlights, ice chest, gig, boat, and paddle, but as far as we know, never made contact with the squirming serpent. We broke off some willow saplings and poled home in the dark, frogless. Neither one of us ever purchased a long paddle after that night.

Somewhere on the banks of Number 12 Drainage Canal there must still stand a monument to this oft-time gigging companion of mine. Troy and I were paddling silently along this canal one night and spotted, as we often did, a big moccasin stalking a bullfrog. I eased his end of the boat toward the bank as he held the two amphibians motionless in the beam of his head-light. Troy expertly gigged the frog literally out from under the snake's nose, and the big moccasin took offense. There on the muddy bank, it coiled and raised its head threateningly at us, hissing like a punctured tire. My friend dropped the frog in the ice chest and responded to the challenge.

We generally used an old hoe-handle for our gigs, because the streams we hunted had soft mud banks and you needed a stout gig to retrieve your catch from six inches deep in Mississippi Delta mud. Troy gigged at the snake's head and he gigged hard. But he missed.

The three-pronged barbed weapon went into the center of the hissing coils and beyond. Ten inches or a foot deep into the clay went the gig, with the last two inches of the moccasin's tail impaled by the middle prong. The viper struck!

A five-foot gig with a five-foot enraged poisonous snake on it doesn't leave much room for the gigger. Troy had reached this conclusion in the nick of time. The snake swarmed up the handle, hissing and twisting in pain. My grand-

151

father was a doctor, so all my life I had seen pictures of a cadeceus, the staff with two serpents entwined upon it that is the physician's symbol. I now gained my first appreciation of the fact that it had wings on top of it.

Two nights later, we ventured back to the spot and found that the snake was still attached to our gig and still bore a grudge toward us. The next night it rained and the canal overflowed. We never went back, and as far as I know, he's still there—waiting!

The Marsh Hunt

Author's Note

As I sorted through this collection of stories trying to decide what order to arrange them in, it slowly dawned on me (admittedly, I'm a slow dawner) that there were two parallel lines here: the life of a man who had been a boy, and the life of a boy who was becoming a man. The threads that bound these two lives together were not so much bloodlines, though there was a common patriarch involved, but lines of friendship. Not the friendship of father to son, however strong that is, but the relationship that somehow develops when older friends of one man become almost foster fathers to that son. I am not convinced that this kinship exists in any association other than the outdoor fraternity.

My own "outdoor uncles" were numerous, and their affect on my life could only be measured by a Higher Authority. Indeed, one Sunday morning when Little Dave and I misbehaved somehow on the front pew, a regular gantlet of those uncles was formed after the closing hymn. Before I made it to the back door, Big Dave, Uncle Shag, Uncle Sam, and Mit'er Mo' all got their licks in to convince me that disrespect to said Higher Authority was not an option open to me. Any attempt to list these men would be incomplete, but they can all be found in *The Flaming Turkey* and *Going Home*.

Similarly, any attempt to list my son Adam's "uncles" would probably end up by leaving someone out, but again, they all appear in these pages. Some have perhaps had more influence than others, but they're all there to be used when needed and he knows that, and that's what counts.

Why do outdoor-type men form these attachments to youngsters? My guess is that on the one hand it's a desire to share their common love of the outdoors with someone just coming along; and also a usually subconscious desire to relive their own departed youth through the eyes of this boy. If your guess is different, don't bother me with it.

In consideration of this subconscious desire, I include a story seen through those young eyes. It was a story written years ago by Adam to enter in a Ducks Unlimited Greenwing Essay Contest, and he won a prize with it. I could not find the final draft, so I admit to doing a rewrite from the handwritten rough draft. But the basic story is that of a youngster with an older friend, Teddy, in this case. But just every one of you, remember: it could be you!

154

Afew years ago in November, Daddy and I went to do some duck hunting in the Louisiana marsh with a friend of ours who lived in New Orleans. Teddy had only one hand, which had been badly burned years before; his other hand was a two-pronged hook which he could open and shut. This handicap doesn't prevent him from hunting and fishing whenever he wants to, as long as Suzanne says it's okay. Daddy had just gotten off crutches from a major knee operation. This made me the only physically healthy person in the bunch.

My family arrived in New Orleans early in the afternoon and we spent the rest of the day visiting with Ted and Suzanne. Later that evening, Ted and I went to a nearby lake to cut some leafy branches for fresh camouflage, which Ted said was the only thing we needed for his marsh blind. When we returned, Daddy helped us hook up Ted's fifteen-foot boat to the truck. Then we loaded all our gear in lidded buckets (which Ted said were also to sit on) and packed them into the boat.

Ted then got me to help him load onto the big boat two tiny things he called pirogues. They were small boats that were shallow draft and short in length. He said they were to carry us from the canal across the marsh to the blind. I had never seen one before.

Suzanne soon called us in for a roast duck dinner, which was delicious. After supper, I helped Ted feed a hearty meal to his black Labrador to prepare her for the next day's hunting trip. Then we all went to bed because we were going to have to get up very early in the morning in order to get to the blind on time.

Sure enough, Teddy shook me awake at 2:30 A.M. and told me to dress lightly because it would be warm. This was a new experience for me since I usually hunt with several layers of clothes because of the cold. We left the house about 3:00 and arrived at the boat launching ramp next to a levee about an hour later, having stopped briefly to pick up coffee, chocolate milk, and doughnuts. I helped Ted unload the boat off the trailer since Daddy couldn't put much weight on his bad leg. Ted then parked the truck and the three of us and the lab got in the boat and started down a small river in the darkness, with Daddy holding the big spotlight.

After motoring several miles, we turned into a narrow channel that led to a small wooden dike across the canal. There we tied the big boat to the dike and unloaded the pirogues and our gear. We divided the stuff between the two little boats, with Teddy taking Daddy, the guns, shells, and dog, and me taking the rest. Since Daddy had to sit with his leg stretched out stiff, Ted intended for me to paddle a pirogue by myself!

I told Ted that this was the first time in my twelve years I had ever seen a pirogue, much less paddled one. He said not to worry, just to take my time while paddling and to be sure not to shift my chewing gum from side to side, and I wouldn't turn over. I think he was joking, but I took him at his word.

I felt uneasy at first, but settled down after I had figured out how to keep my balance in the tipsy little boat. Teddy led the way, Daddy holding the flashlight, and I followed through the many winding channels in the marsh, concentrating on staying upright. I still don't know how he found his way through the marsh in the dark. Several times I fell behind and lost sight of them, and then I'd yell for them to shine the light toward me and slow down. I also ran up on the bank a few times and almost capsized the pirogue.

Finally, after what seemed to be an eternity, we arrived at the blind and began to set out the decoys. The blind itself was a four-foot by six-foot piece of marsh in the middle of a three-acre pond into which several canals led. A wooden pallet formed the floor of the blind to keep us from sinking into the muck, and it was surrounded by brushy cedar limbs. Before we entered the blind, Ted warned us to look out for snakes. I couldn't believe snakes would be out during duck season.

Teddy put Daddy and me and all the gear out at the blind and took the second pirogue to hide it in the marsh. He returned shortly and I helped him camouflage his boat behind the blind, while the dog positioned herself in front. Then we got into the blind and loaded our guns. Now we were ready for ducks. Ted and Daddy had agreed that I would get first shot on any ducks that came in. I could hardly wait for daylight.

Soon it was light enough to shoot, and we could see literally hundreds of ducks flying toward us. One flock of pintails came straight into us with their wings cupped. Ted and I had our guns in hand while Daddy's leaned against the blind. His past experience with pintails was that they circled several times before coming in, but that was not the case this time. They decoyed straight to my side of the blind and I dropped the lead drake. The dog hit the water for the retrieve almost at the same time. I saw the duck was crippled, but he was too close to shoot again, so my hopes were with the dog. The duck seemed to watch calmly as the lab closed in, then dived just as the retriever opened her mouth. He just never came back up.

I can still picture the majestic duck in the few seconds he sat on the water by me. All of his feathers were defined and his grey pin tail made him look kingly. I was really upset to lose the first pintail I had ever shot.

Shortly, another flight of pintails came in and this time we were all ready. Three dropped, but one more crippled off and fell almost a quarter mile away in the water. Ted got in the pirogue to look for him since it was too far to send the dog. While he was gone, yet another flock of pins came in and I got one. A few minutes later some wigeons decoyed and I knocked one down in the marsh to our right. Then Ted returned with the ugliest duck I have ever seen. He said it was an immature pintail drake. His feathers were greyish, even his neck and chest. He didn't have a pin tail and his wings looked partially plucked. He was a far cry from the first beautiful drake that had gotten away.

By this time, the sun was fully up and we could see clearly all around us. I noticed several different species trading from place to place: pintails, mallards, shovelers, ring-necks, both blue and green-wing teal, and others I didn't recognize. This many species was a real change for Daddy and me, because in the Mississippi Delta we were used to seeing mostly mallards and wood ducks, with a few wigeons and gadwalls, and an occasional pintail.

The first blue-winged teal I ever killed came in next. We were scanning the sky and failed to notice a pair of teal that came zipping down a canal just above the water and dropped right into our decoys. Teddy and I quickly stood up and got both of them. When the dog had retrieved them, I examined the colorful drake. His wing bar was a beautiful irridescent blue and white. The white around his eyes formed a quarter moon shape.

A few minutes later, another duck slipped in and sat in the decoys. When I stood to shoot, he exploded from the water and flew directly toward me, veering to the right just before I shot. I led him perfectly and he dropped like a rock. He was so close, I almost shot him up too badly. Once we got the duck in the blind, I couldn't figure out what it was, until Ted showed me the white ring around his neck that of course meant a ring-neck duck. Then we dropped two mallards and crippled another before Ted said it was time to go home.

He took me to get the pirogue that he had hidden in the marsh. Luckily, it was close to where one of our cripples had fallen. I asked Ted if I could go look for it, and he said yes, but cautioned me to walk on top of the reeds so I wouldn't sink into the mushy ground underneath. When I found where the

158

duck had fallen, I stepped up on a muskrat lodge to look for it, and sure enough, there it was next to another lodge. But as I stepped off the mound, I fell through the reeds and disappeared from the two men's sight. The muck lacked about two inches being over my waders. Carefully, I pulled myself back up onto the reeds and picked up the duck, holding it in the air to let them know I had found it. When I got the pirogue and paddled to the blind, they identified it as a gadwall hen.

We loaded up the pirogues, and this time Daddy decided to try to paddle one while Ted took me and the dog. I was treated to an old fashioned push-pole ride to the big boat. I had been barely able to keep my balance while sitting down and paddling on the way out. Now Ted stood perfectly balanced in the stern and poled us along at a fast clip with only one hand. Even so, we quickly outdistanced Daddy and had to stop several times to let him catch up. He had a hard time keeping his balance because of the position of his leg, and when we reached the motorboat, his pirogue had a good bit of water in it.

On our way, I noticed several strange noises. One sounded like a cat meowing. I asked Ted what it was and he replied that it was a muskrat.

After we returned to the levee boat landing and loaded the boat on the trailer, Teddy got his camera and took pictures. Now I have in my album these memories of a most exciting adventure in the Louisiana Marsh.

Going Home

The echos of the ambulance siren's wail hung over the small town like smoke from an extinguished fire. . . .

He woke slowly, easing gradually into consciousness. His head felt full, heavy, "kinda cobwebby," he mused drowsily. He pushed up on one elbow, flinching involuntarily as his funny bone momentarily rested against a twelve gauge shell that had spilled from his hunting coat.

"Maankind!" he drawled, "I sho' musta slep hard!" He shook his head to clear it, rubbing his eyes with a fist that seemed to be more sensitive than usual. "Gettin' more feelin' back in these fingers every day," he thought.

The trickling sound that had punctuated his dreamless trance came from a small, clay-bottomed branch that sent its leaf-stained waters flowing busily around a sassafras shoot that had caved off the foot-high bank during the last rain, though its roots clung doggedly to the mother sapling. The brook was close enough for him to roll to his knees, doff his old camouflage cap, and dip a billful of the cool, clear fluid. He drank several billfuls, holding the cap bill cupped with the topside up. A slight grin made his blue eyes sparkle as he thought, "Wist I had a nickle for ever' gallon-a this stuff me an' ole Crawford have drunk!" The blue eyes misted up a little, "Wist he was drinkin' outa this branch with me now."

A search of his hunting coat pockets turned up one sausage and biscuit wrapped in waxed paper. He sat on the side of the branch with his knees drawn up, one long arm propped over the knee, the huge work-roughened

163

hand dangling idly while he ate slowly, taking small bites so as to savour the spicy home-made sausage more.

"Don't 'member when a sausage 'n biscuit tasted so good," he reflected. He saved the last bite for Freckles, who was undoubtedly curled up on the sunny side of the sand blow about twenty yards up the branch, carefully folded the wax paper up in his pocket, and washed the small meal down with another couple of cap bills of water.

The old Remington pump was leaning breeched against the sassafras sapling. Using it as a crutch, he laboriously heaved himself to his feet, noting with a little surprise that the old bad leg didn't seem to be as completely asleep as he expected. Still leaning on the Remington, though, he stomped his foot several times routinely to try to restore what circulation he still had left in the leg.

"Freckles! Heah!" he called to the still unseen pointer.

As he watched for the dog to appear, he absentmindedly searched first his shirt pockets, then the hunting coat pockets, for an after-lunch cigarette. He patted the side pants pockets, also unsuccessfully—not even a lighter. A glance around him failed to locate the missing items. "Musta' mislaid 'em someplace," he shrugged, mildly wondering that he wasn't irritated and that the nicotine urge wasn't too strong right now.

His search was interrupted anyway by a small sized, but surprisingly plump, liver and white spotted blur that shot through a sedge grass clearing, bounded across the branch and pounced frenziedly against his chest with muddy forepaws. The pointer gulped the proffered bite of sausage and biscuit, licking the man's hand joyously, his tail busily slapping each boot top in turn.

"You ole scoun'nel," grinned the man as he scratched the briar-torn ear, "fella would think you ain't seen me in fifteen years!" The dog moaned his pleasure, pushing his head harder into the caressing hand.

Man and dog stood hugging each other in total communion for a long

164

unmoving loving minute. Then the man tugged mock-roughly on the torn ear. "C'mon, you ole rabbit-runner," he grinned, swallowing a strange lump in his throat, "le's see can you point a bird."

He always enjoyed watching Freckles start off, speeding in wide looping circles such as he now began on the other side of the branch. "Fastest dog in the country," he bragged to himself, "goes like a striped ape!"

The old bad leg didn't give him the trouble he had expected in crossing the little branch, and he slipped three shells in the old Remington as he started across the sedge grass field toward the creek. "B'lieve that's the south fork of Polutia Creek, but this ridge don't seem quite as steep as I remembered," he thought. "Too much of a nap, I guess, but I'll pick up my bearings in a minute. Look at that scoun'nel go!"

The liver-and-white had already made a loop midway the ridge and now was circling back to the top, framed against the hazy fall sky. He passed the edge of a post oak thicket, head high, and made a beeline for a bunch of chinaberry trees marking an old house site. Suddenly he braked, looking like he was trying to walk on eggs, made a few steps to his left and froze, pointing in a small dewberry patch. He was perfectly silouetted on the top of the ridge, a picture from a bird hunter's paradise.

"Hold!" the man shouted, knowing as he yelled it was unnecessary. "Holds his head too low, an' I reckon he always will wag that tail real slow, but he'll hold a point 'til Hell freezes over."

The short climb was not as hard as he had thought it would be. He had expected the dragging foot to catch on more of the dewberry vines that trailed here and there. He wasn't even breathing real hard when he topped the ridge.

The whites of Freckles' eyes showed as he cut them around without turning his head to check on his boss man. "I'm gettin' there, fella," the man assured him, "I'm just enjoyin' the picture." The pointer had the birds at the edge of

165

another sedge grass field that stretched down the other side of the ridge to the creek a hundred yards away. The post oak thicket to his right, a deep gully on the left, bounded the field. "Perfect spot!" he thought. "They'll get up, sail across the sedge, an' the singles'll drop in t'other side a'th' creek."

He stood for a moment caressing the safety of the old pump gun, lost in just the simple enjoyment of watching the little pointer, whose tail continued that slow wag. Freckles cut his eyes around to glance at the hunter again and moaned softly. The man took a deep breath, savouring the smell of ripe muscadines mixed with the left-over smoke from someone's early morning fire. "The autumn of a man's life" he thought, "ought to smell like ripe muscadines, woodsmoke, gun oil, and dogs. I ain't appreciated them like this in a while. That's a good thought. I'm glad I thunk it."

"Okay, Podnuh," he spoke softly to the impatient dog.

As he stepped in front of the pointer, the ground exploded and a dozen bob-white whirred up in a perfect fan over the sedge grass field. The heavy gun seemed to shoulder itself, the safety snicked as it came up, and the barrel almost lazily swung past a cock-bird, which crumpled at the single report.

"Small covey," the hunter told his companion. "One's enough." Freckles told him with a look that he not only understood, but concurred, and would try not to point any more small coveys. He retrieved the still-fluttering bird lovingly and brought it to the man, who accepted it the same way. The rough hands smoothed the brown feathers for a moment, then started to slip the quivering form into the game pocket. There was a sudden whirr of wings and both man and dog started with surprise as the quail escaped the transfer from hand to coat and buzzed down the hillside to join his mates.

"Musta just been stunned," the man grinned ruefully at the dog. " 'At's aw'right. Let him go. We had our fun with him."

166

Freckles started toward the creek that the singles had crossed, but the hunter called him back.

"Let 'em go," he ordered, and hand-motioned the pointer toward the west. "Sun's gittin' low fast, boy, and we need to be headin' on home."

His chest felt kind of full and that lump in his throat was there again. He caught himself moving too closely behind the dog and had to make a conscious effort to slow down. "Pushin' th' dog too much. Huntin' just like ole Albert used to," he chided himself.

The two of them were heading down the ridgetop toward the setting sun, Freckles not hunting as hard now, but still on the lookout for a covey close to their route. "That dog just knows!" he thought.

A cowbell tinkled on a far-off ridge, and somewhere a woman tapped a spoon on the bottom of a dishpan to call her menfolks to knock off and wash up. "Like Mama used to do," he mused. 'Way down the ridge they were walking a hound suddenly gave voice.

"Aaaah-rooooohp!" the hound trumpeted, "Aaaah-rooooohp!"

"Thas's ole Jupiter!" the man exclaimed to the little pointer. "Got him a fox or a rabbit, one. Or mebbe he's just callin' us. Betcha ole Gabriel wisht he could blow like that," he chuckled.

The pointer made a sweep around the edge of a big thicket of blackjack oaks up ahead. "If you gonna find anoth'n, you better git on it 'fore ole Jupe gits here," the hunter called to his dog. "Way he bellows, ever'thing for a quarter mile each side of 'im's gonna run!"

The black-and-tan belled again, and the man shook his head in admiration. "Fust time I heard him, he sounded just like that, an' him just a pint-sized pup. Seems like twenty-five years ago," he paused. "Naw, couldn't be. Where does time go?"

167

The sun seemed to be setting extra fast today, he thought. The liver-and-white checked the edge of a thick stand of cedars down the other side of the ridge from the blackjack oaks with no results. Wheeling, he loped down the old road on the ridgetop between the cedars and oaks and disappeared from sight. In the distance, but drawing closer, the hound belled.

The man knew he had never walked this old wagon track before, yet somehow he knew there was one more sedge grass field on the other side of the thickets. "Thas's where this ridge points out," he thought, "and then it's downhill all the way to Home".

Jupiter bayed again down the ridge, and suddenly the hunter was overcome by a tremendous longing to Be There. His chest seemed so full he could hardly breathe, yet he realized he had broken into a light-footed walking-trot. He willed himself to slow down, "Gonna trip and bust myself wide open!" he opined. Yet the baying hound seemed to draw him with invisible strings around his swelling heart. "Reckon I jus' love that voice!" he said softly.

He broke out of the narrow lane through the trees into the clearing he had known about. Freckles had obviously cased the north side of the field, and was crossing the ridge again at the high point on the other end of the sedge grass. The dog swung suddenly, nose high, and advanced cautiously to the end of the ridge, where a huge pecan tree and a tumbledown old chimney marked a former residence. He sank lower to the ground and his tail started its telltale wag just as he went out of sight behind what was left of an old privet hedge.

"Hold!" the man yelled automatically, and broke into a half-run. "Gonna be a contest whether me or Jupiter gits there first!" he thought. He realized, feeling rather foolish, that his gait had become a run, and once again willed himself to slow down. "Lord, I ain't run since th' time lightnin' hit that tree I was under back during turkey season! 'Sides, there ain't a steadier bird-dog in th' South."

168

He rounded the privet bushes to behold not one, but two liver and white statues on point. The only time Freckles did not wag his tail while pointing was when he was honoring another dog. Thirty yards in front of the pointer was a smaller dog, a little longer of hair, her smaller spots sprinkled a little more liberally than his.

"A drop," thought the man, using the local name for a setter-pointer crossbreed. She looked familiar to him. He realized it was Queen just before he heard the voice from over the rise.

"Birds, Queen! Birds!"—the man knew it was Crawford's voice before the grinning face appeared over the rise.—"Theah they are. Hold! Ain't that a pichure?"

The hunter nodded dumbly in agreement. The two dogs stood rigid in the gathering dusk and the two old friends gazed fondly at them for a long moment. Crawford broke the spell.

"C'mon, le's jump these pottiges. It's about quittin' time anyway." He clucked his tongue and Queen pounced into the middle of the covey. It was a large one and the little brown bombshells burst all around her and whirred off toward the creek. The two dogs touched noses and loped together over the rise. Jupiter belled again in that direction, close.

"I kinda figgered you'd be comin' thisaway, so I asked 'em to let me meet you," Crawford grinned. "Home's just a little piece over that rise."

The man emptied his pump and shouldered it. Jupiter's baying seemed to come directly from the setting sun, which hung over the rise. His chest felt swelled to the bursting point with a strange type of joyous anticipation. He took a deep breath of the autumn smells and spoke around that lump in his throat.

"Well, le's go Home!"

169

The doctor's mask hung around his neck and he spread his hands wide as he approached the family. "Sometimes you do everything you can and it's still not enough!" he tried to explain wearily. "Sometimes you just have to let 'em go."

"It's over? He's gone?" the younger brother asked with a half-sob.

"It's over. He's gone." repeated the doctor dejectedly. "You know, I was crazy about him, too."

"It's okay, Doc," the older brother soothed. "He wouldn't have wanted to go on without being able to get out and around. He's probably better off."

The younger brother blew his nose. "Well, we better go tell the girls," he sighed.

The three friends walked together in silence out the front of the small-town hospital. As they reached the sidewalk, the baying of a far-off hound could be heard faintly. The doctor broke the silence.

"Sounds like that old black-and-tan y'all used to have when y'all were kids," he remarked.

"Old Jupiter?" the older brother asked.

"Lordee, Doc," the younger one said, "what made you think of him? That's been twenty-five years ago!"

The Broken Mold

The van full of pallbearers pulled up behind us and Teddy caught me as I walked around the car to get Mother out.

"When you get your Mother settled, come on down to the store," he spoke softly. "Me and Micky are gonna show you rednecks how to have a wake."

Half an hour later I walked into the old plantation commissary. I had never attended a wake before and was not prepared for the scene I beheld. Someone had thrown a blanket over an old table and found a deck of cards. A double handful of roofing nails had been distributed for chips. Several bottles and an ice bucket sat on a counter and the door to the drink machine was standing open. A cooler of beer sat on the floor.

Charlie, Russ, Beau, Dude, and Micky sat around the table with cards in front of them. S. P. and David perched on stools behind the players. Teddy dangled his legs from the counter where he guarded the bottles. He handed me a plastic cup with a couple of ounces of very good cognac in it.

"Wow! Where'd this come from?" I coughed after a sip. Teddy pointed with his cup at the supine form of Mountain Willy in the creaky old glider on the other side of the card game.

"How's your Mama?" Willy wanted to know.

"She'll be okay, I guess. Worn out right now," I answered. I realized that the card players were kinda laid back about their game. The cards seemed to be just an excuse for sitting around and talking.

Dude picked up the story my entrance had interrupted. "Anyway, Bob and

173

Beau finally drove up in the Ghost and Big Robert near about ran out on the porch to meet them. 'Looka here,' he told them, 'Dude's made me listen to how he killed that li'l ole turkey nine times in two hours! Now y'all listen to the son-of-a-gun for a while. I'm goin' over to the Drunk Cabin!' "

The chuckles were subdued. Charlie began to shuffle the cards and everybody pointedly did not look at Dude as he wiped an eye with the edge of the blanket.

Beau nodded, "He was like that. But I remember one time he was just the opposite." He looked at Russ. "Weren't you over there the time he killed that great big nine-point the morning Bob and I had gone duck hunting?" Russ grinned assent and Beau continued, "We finally came back to the cabin, half-drowned, and Big Robert said 'Where the hell have y'all been? I've been waitin' two hours for somebody to brag to!' "

His voice had a quaver at the last of the story and he got up abruptly and turned to the counter for a beer. I guessed that a wake must be where you sit around and talked about good memories you had shared with your departed companion. Teddy confirmed my intuition. "Funerals are usually sad," he stated. "Wakes are where you're sorry you're not gonna have somebody around anymore, but you're glad you were able to be part of his life." He paused and reflected, "I reckon they're sad, too, in a way. But they're happy, too." He raised his voice and addressed the group, "He musta been glad when I went back to Louisiana after I killed my first turkey, 'cause there ain't no tellin' how many times he listened to me tell it. Matter of fact, he even asked me to tell it to Mr. Drunk one more time!"

"He knew you needed to brag," Charlie said. "He figured anybody had hunted that long without killin' a turkey had some braggin' to catch up on!"

"Yeah, he knew when you needed to talk and when he needed to shut you

174

up," Dude added. "You know, he coulda just brought up the year before when you shot outa shells!"

"He did, finally," Ted confessed ruefully.

"Don't feel like the Lone Ranger!" Russ laughed brokenly, "He'd always bring up all those deer I missed my first time on the island whenever I'd get too big for my britches."

S. P. sighed and turned his head away, "It sure won't be the same over there without him. They broke the mold after they made that one!"

There were nods of agreement in the silence that followed. Dude got up and walked to the window. Mountain Willy stared mistily at the ceiling. Charlie dealt a hand that included a full house to Micky and a straight flush to Beau. The ensuing flurry of roofing tacks lightened the mood a little.

"Wish we were all on the island," remarked Dude from the window.

"Yeah, that'd be perfect for the occasion," agreed S. P. "That place feels more like home than home does."

"How long has Bob been carrying you over there?" Beau asked him, "Twenty-five years?"

S. P. snorted, "How long has Bob been carrying me over there? You and Bob ain't been members but about ten years! Who do you think started invitin' me? Big Robert was the one guested me!"

"That's right!" Russ declared. "All the time you two were gone to college and the service, he would take me with him a couple of times a year."

Micky nodded, "Actually, for the first few years y'all were back, the other members thought y'all were my guests 'cause I'd been there so much the years y'all were gone."

Mountain Willy observed softly to the ceiling, "He always wrote me of his boys,' meaning the whole bunch of you. For a lot of years he could have been huntin' with his friends his age, but he went out of his way to take guys his sons' ages."

David took Dude's seat at the table. "Deal!" he ordered Russ roughly.

Charlie took a deep breath, "I ever tell y'all about the time he taught me how to turkey call? He put me on one side of the tree. . . ."

I gave Dude a punch on the arm as I went by him on the way to the bathroom. Closing the door, I cut the water on to drown out Charlie's story and sat on the side of the tub with a towel. I needed one to think back over the events of the last couple of days.

Those men in the other room had begun arriving the afternoon before. I had phoned them the news of the death and the time of the services. I had not told any of them that today was my son's fourteenth birthday. It was poor scheduling, but unavoidable because of out-of-town kinfolks and friends. I had apologized and tried to explain to him, but in the end his "uncles" had done better than I had.

It started with The Mick, who had flown in from a thousand miles away. After all the hugging and kissing from the womenfolks was over, I had helped him bring his baggage in.

"Got a little something for the boy," he declared. "Bring me some oil and a rag and we'll wipe it down." He pulled a long flat box with "Ruger" on it out of his duffle bag. I made the connection instantly. Micky had gone with us for the first deer season and knew that Adam had been saving for a new Ruger 10/22. The kid had gone around to all the other cabins asking them to save all the empty beer and drink cans for him.

"Aw, Man, that's nice!" I exclaimed as he opened the box. "What're you gonna do, let him pay you what he's got and owe you the rest? He must have close to ninety dollars now."

176

"This ain't for sellin', it's for givin'," Micky demurred. "Ain't tomorrow his birthday?"

"Yeah, but this is too much to give him. Lemme go halvers with you."

"Nope."

"Micky, I can't let you give him that new gun."

"I didn't ask you!" my bearded friend spoke with a sudden intensity. "This ain't none of your business! This is 'tween me and Adam. Listen! If it's up to his Uncle Micky, that boy will remember tomorrow for something besides the day they buried his grandaddy!"

"You son-of-a-gun!" I choked, and grabbed the burly shoulders. You don't have to be a kid to cry on somebody's shoulder.

Teddy had shown up later with a fishing cap full of fishing lures. Beau asked permission to give an H & R long-barreled .22 pistol to a fourteen-year-old. Russ or Charlie one slipped him a belt knife the next day, his birthday. Dude came in with his compound bow and a quiver of arrows and told Adam he was unable to shoot it anymore since his back operation. "So I might as well let another southpaw have it," he had said. Someone, S. P. I think, laid a roll of silver dollars on the kid's dresser upstairs. Dan presented him with a baseball autographed by a former big leaguer, now a famous college coach. As far as I know, none of this had been planned.

Strange thing was, as much as all of it meant to that fourteen-year-old, it probably meant more to me.

I know one act did.

One of Adam's classmates had been thoughty enough to bring his books and assignments home so he could catch up on the three days he had missed. Mark caught Adam after the funeral to say he had the books at his house. Russ happened to overhear Adam's reply: "I'll get somebody to bring me in to get them." Russ volunteered to take the boy into town when we all returned from the cemetary.

When I left Mother's house to walk home and change out of a coat and tie before going to the Store, Russ fell in step beside me.

"Adam talked any about his Granddaddy's death yet?" he asked gently.

"Not a word," I said, "it's really tough on the kid. Big Robert was probably his best friend as well as Granddaddy, and then this being his birthday, too," I paused. "I tried to explain things to him, but as far as I know, he's still got it all bottled up, and that ain't good."

"Well, we stopped and talked awhile on the way back from Mark's," Russ said. "Don't worry about him. He got it out of his system and I think he's okay now."

I rubbed my coat sleeve across my eyes and managed to whisper, "Thanks." We walked the rest of the way in silence.

Now I stood up and cut the water off.

Charlie had just finished his story in a round of sad-but-happy laughter and one or two snuffles. Now he, too, sighed and repeated S. P.'s earlier statement, "They sho' don't make 'em like that any more. They've broken that mold!"

I had to grin as I stepped back into the big room. I wanted to shout what I had just realized, but I chickened out and muttered to myself. "Oh, yes, they do make 'em like that some more, Charlie. And I betcha they're still using the same old mold!"